Rethinking the transition process in Syria: constitution, participation and gender equality

Edited by Claudia Padovani and Francesca Helm

Research-publishing.net

Research-publishing.net

Published by Research-publishing.net, not-for-profit association
Voillans, France, info@research-publishing.net

Rethinking the transition process in Syria: constitution, participation and gender equality
Edited by Claudia Padovani and Francesca Helm

Disclaimer: Research-publishing.net does not take any responsibility for the content of the pages written by the authors of this book. The authors have recognised that the work described was not published before, or that it was not under consideration for publication elsewhere. While the information in this book are believed to be true and accurate on the date of its going to press, neither the editorial team, nor the publisher can accept any legal responsibility for any errors or omissions that may be made. The publisher makes no warranty, expressed or implied, with respect to the material contained herein. While Research-publishing.net is committed to publishing works of integrity, the words are the authors' alone.
Also, this report has been produced with the financial support of the European Union and Sweden. The contents of this document are the sole responsibility of the writers and can under no circumstances be regarded as reflecting the position of the European Union or Sweden.

Trademark notice: product or corporate names may be trademarks or registered trademarks, and are used only for identification and explanation without intent to infringe.

Copyrighted material: every effort has been made by the editorial team to trace copyright holders and to obtain their permission for the use of copyrighted material in this book. In the event of errors or omissions, please notify the publisher of any corrections that will need to be incorporated in future editions of this book.

Typeset by Research-publishing.net
Cover design by © Raphaël Savina (raphael@savina.net)

ISBN13: 978-2-490057-07-8 (Ebook, PDF, colour)
ISBN13: 978-2-490057-08-5 (Ebook, EPUB, colour)
ISBN13: 978-2-490057-06-1 (Paperback - Print on demand, black and white)
Print on demand technology is a high-quality, innovative and ecological printing method; with which the book is never 'out of stock' or 'out of print'.

Legal deposit, United Kingdom: The British Library.
British Library Cataloguing-in-Publication Data.
A cataloguing record for this book is available from the British Library.

Legal deposit, France: Bibliothèque Nationale de France - Dépôt légal: avril 2018.

Table of contents

Section 1.

Transitional justice from a gender-sensitive perspective: CEDAW and UN Resolution 1325

Section 2.

The role of women in the Syrian uprising and in the political transitional process

Section 3.

Launching the ABC for a gender sensitive constitution

Section 4.

Testimonies by civil society organizations and Syrian lawyers' internships at the CIRSG and SPGI

Notes on contributors

Editors

Claudia Padovani is Senior Lecturer in Political Science and International Relations at the University of Padova (Italy) where she teaches courses in International Communication and Politics of the Global Societies. She is the Director of the University Interdepartmental Center for Gender Studies (CIRSG). Padovani is amongst the founders of the Mapping Global Media Policy digital platform and a co-chair of the Working Group on Global Media Policy at the IAMCR. She is an active member of the UNESCO-promoted Global Alliance for Media and Gender, and one of the coordinators of the UNESCO Unitwin Network on Gender Media and ICT. Her main areas of interest concern the transformation of political processes in the global context and their connection to the evolution of communication dynamics and technologies, with a special focus on gender, communication rights, and social justice.

Francesca Helm is an assistant professor at the Department of Politics, Law and International Studies at the University of Padova, Italy, where she teaches English. She is co-founder of the Next Generation Global Studies initiative and vice-chair of the Education Innovation working group of the Coimbra Group of Universities.

Authors

Maya Alrahabi is a Syrian physician who practiced and taught medicine between 1978-2010, after which she became the director of Musawa/Women Studies Center, as well as the manager of Alrahbi Publishing House for feminist publications and the director of several women empowerment projects in Syria and Lebanon. She is a feminist and a political activist and author. Her publications include Islam and Women (2013), Feminism: Concepts and Issues (2014), and a novel, Furat (2000), in addition to multiple published researches and lectures on women in Arab societies and women's rights. Between 2001 and 2004, Maya Alrahabi was a coordinating member for "Committees for the Revival of Civil Society" in Syria, and between 2004-2010 the president of "Maan" (Together) for supporting women issues. She currently works as the information coordinator for the Coalition of Syrian Women for Democracy (CSWD) and a member of the Syrian Feminist Lobby (SFL).

Roula Baghdadi is an attorney in law and human rights lawyer, working in Syria since 2007, mainly on human rights and gender issues. She has worked on several researches concerning the legal dimension of gender equality, constitutional challenges in Syria, and sexual violence against Syrian women in the context of international law. She served as the head of the legal team of the Syrian NGO Equal Citizenship Centre (ECC) working on legal cases for abused Syrian women for more than four years and is a member of the directors' board at the ECC since November 2016. She has been studying her Master's degree in Public Law in Beirut Arab University since September 2016.

Francesco Biagi is a Senior Research Fellow at the Max Planck Foundation for International Peace and the Rule of Law (Heidelberg), and Researcher at the Center for Constitutional Studies and Democratic Development (Bologna). Between 2012 and 2015, he was a Postdoctoral Research Fellow at the University of Bologna's School of Law. He obtained a Ph.D. in Constitutional Law from the University of Ferrara after graduating in Law from the University of Bologna. In 2012, his research on "Constitutional Courts in Democratic Transitions: The Cases of Italy, Spain and the Czech Republic" was awarded best Ph.D. thesis in Constitutional Law at the University of Ferrara by the Istituto Universitario di Studi Superiori (IUSS). In March 2015 he was Visiting Professor at the College of Law of the University of Illinois. His latest publications include: *Corti costituzionali e transizioni democratiche. Tre generazioni a confronto*, il Mulino, Bologna 2016; *Political and Constitutional Transitions in North Africa: Actors and Factors*, Routledge, London 2015, edited with Justin O. Frosini; *The Separation and Distribution of Powers Under the New Moroccan Constitution*, in R. Grote, T. J. Röder (eds.); and *Constitutionalism, Human Rights and Islam after the Arab Spring*, Oxford University Press, Oxford 2016 (forthcoming).

Paola Degani is Aggregate Professor of Public Policies and Human Rights at Degree Course in Political Science, International Relations, Human Rights and of Women's Human rights in the Master's degree in Human Rights and Multi-Level Governance. She is a scientific coordinator and member of the technical and scientific committees and trainer of many EU projects on trafficking of human beings and acts for stronger private-public partnerships in the field of identification and support of child victims and people at risk of trafficking in Europe through: Save the Children, Austria, Greece, Italy and Romania (AGIRE); AgainST emerging fOrms of trafficking in Italy: exPloited immigrants in the international phenomenon of FORced BEGgging (STOP FOR BEG); Trafficked and Exploited Minors between Vulnerability and Illegality (TEMVI); and forced criminal activities as a new form of exploitation in human trafficking: knowledge and human rights based practices through pilot research and multi-agency training and prototype-procedures. Main scientific areas of interest: women's rights and equal opportunities; international system of promotion and protection of women's rights; violence against women as violations of human rights; gender security; gender dimension of the intercultural dialog; trafficking of human beings especially for the purpose of sexual exploitation; policies on prostitution and trafficking related issues; mixed flows: refugees as trafficked persons and trafficked persons as asylum claims or refugees; and children's rights.

Giulia D'Odorico is a gender expert (Ph.D. Sociology, MA Governance and Development, BA International Relations) with a focus on SGBV and sexual and reproductive rights; she conducted research on gender, SGBV, migration, and development issues in Democratic Republic of Congo, Belgium, Ecuador, Morocco, and Italy for MA and doctoral studies, Amnesty International Belgique, the UN, and the University of Padova. She was with the NGO Associazione Trama di terre since 2015 as a coordinator of a refugee reception center aimed at women and children victims of SGBV and trafficking in Italy.

Ibrahim Draji is a professor in international law. For ten years, he has been working on issues of trafficking in persons and refugees in Syria and the Arab World, previously with the International Organization for Migration, and currently with the UN High Commissioner for Refugees. He has written numerous papers published by international organizations on these issues. Since

2011, he has been working on legal protection within the mission of the UN High Commissioner for Refugees in Syria. He is the co-writer of the "ABC for a Gender Sensitive Constitution" published by Euromed Feminist Initiative in 2015.

Massimiliano Fanni Canelles is a journalist and doctor. Director of the monthly magazine "SocialNews", under RAI. Professor at the University of Bologna in international cooperation. Foreign policy, and human rights expert. He is invited as expert in national television broadcasts (LA7, RAI, SKY, Mediaset) and is also the founder and President of @uxilia Foundation. Has taken part in several humanitarian missions in Syria, Iraq, Afghanistan, Pakistan, Africa, Sri Lanka, and South-East Asia. Director of care center of Nephrology and Dialysis in Integrated Health Service University in Cividale, he holds a Degree in Medicine and Surgery; Massimiliano Fanni Canelles is also president of the Italian Myelin Project Committee that funds research on rare and demyelinating diseases.

Lilian Halls French worked the largest part of her professional life as a researcher. She has been teaching sociology for some years in Vietnam. She has been professionally involved in the political sphere as an adviser on women's rights for different ministers in France. Lilian Halls French is now Co-President of the Euromed Feminist Initiative IFE-IFE, and an author and co-author of several studies and publications in the field of women's rights. She participated in the reference group for the development of "ABC for a Gender Sensitive Constitution".

Mariam Jalabi was born in Damascus, Syria, and raised in the Golan Heights. She has served as Director for the National Coalition of Syrian Revolution and Opposition Forces' Representative Office to the United Nations since 2013. She has been actively involved in politics and democratic advocacy since before the start of peaceful demonstrations in Syria, and has led events and rallies in support of the Syrian revolution in the US and Canada. She is a founding member of the Syrian Non-Violence Movement (SNVM) and participated in the formation of the Syrian National Council (SNC). Ms. Jalabi is a member of the

Syrian Women Network and the Syrian Feminist Lobby. She has spearheaded numerous projects and initiatives to expand the political participation of Syrian women and minorities, as well as increase their presence in the media. Mariam Jalabi is an independent business owner with degrees in Political Science from McGill University in Montreal and Fashion Design from FIT in New York. True to what Syria represents, she has a rich multi-ethnic, cultural background and is fluent in English, Arabic, and Circassian.

Lama Kannout is a Syrian political and women's rights activist. She holds a B.A. in interior design and owns and manages Lama Advertising Agency since 1992. She was a member of the political office of the Arab Socialists Movement (2000-2008) and has co-founded several civil society organisations. In addition, she is an executive office member of the Musawa Organization since 2012, chairperson of the board of directors of the Syrian Center for Citizenship since 2013, and the coordinator of the studies committee in the Syrian Feminist Lobby since its establishment on the 15/07/2014. Lama Kannout is also a member of the executive committee of the Coalition of Syrian Women for Democracy (CSWD). During the year 2014, she worked with various CSWD members on a project to engender the Syrian constitution. The project concluded with three publications on a gendered constitution building process for Syria. Lama. Kannout has participated in the indirect talks of Geneva II in 2014 as a member of the follow-up committee of the Syrian Women for Peace and Democracy Initiative. Additionally, she participated in writing the NGO shadow report to the Committee on the Elimination of all Discrimination Against Women (CEDAW) in response to the Government report on Syria.

Annalisa Oboe is Vice Rector for Cultural, Social, and Gender Relations of the University of Padova, Italy. She is Professor of English Literature and Postcolonial Studies and currently coordinates the doctoral program in Linguistic, Philological and Literary Sciences at DiSLL. Her research focuses on postcolonial theory and cultures, South African and Black Atlantic literatures, and British colonial and contemporary literature. Among her publications are Experiences of Freedom in Postcolonial Literatures and Cultures (Routledge, 2011); Recharting the Black Atlantic: Modern Cultures, Local Communities,

Global Connections (Routledge, 2008); Mongrel Signatures. Reflections on the Work of Mudrooroo (Rodopi, 2003); and Fiction, History and Nation in South Africa (Supernova, 1994). She is P.I. and coordinator of the research project Postcolonialitalia, and editor of the new periodical From the European South: a transdisciplinary journal of postcolonial humanities (issue 1, 2016).

Sara Pennicino is Assistant Professor of Comparative Public Law at the University of Padova, Italy, where she teaches Human Rights Monitoring and Electoral Observation and Constitutional Development and Democratization. After completing a Ph.D. in Comparative Public Law (2008) at the University of Siena, she became a first year postdoctoral research fellow at the University of Bologna's School of Law. In the meantime, she also became an affiliated scholar of the Center for Constitutional Studies and Democratic Development, a research partnership between the School of Law of the University of Bologna and the Johns Hopkins University Paul H. Nitze School of Advanced International Studies in Bologna, Italy (SAIS Europe), where to date she holds the position of Research Fellow. She is the author of numerous articles published in Italian and international law reviews focusing on American constitutional law, Election Law, Electoral Justice and is a member of the Board of Reviewers of Comparative Legilinguistics (Journal for International Legal Communication). Her current academic work addresses the role played by electoral watchdog bodies in transitional and post-conflict countries, with particular reference to countries that were assisted by the international community in organizing and conducting elections on the one hand, and solving electoral disputes on the other. The mother of a baby girl, she lives in Bologna, Italy.

Yousef Razouk is a Ph.D. student in Public Law with Specialism in Constitutional and Electoral Studies, and got a Master's Degree in Public Law (Constitutional and Electoral Studies) from Damascus University, Syria. Yousef is a lawyer and researcher in the field of gender equality and public freedoms. He is also the voluntary coordinator of the research team at the Equal Citizenship Center which is a voluntary NGO focusing on gender equality and women's empowerment. Additionally, he is a voluntary Gender Expert at the Aga Khan Foundation.

Francesca Rondina joined IFE-EFI in May 2015 as Program Officer and provides project administration and logistics coordination. Francesca has experience in reports drafting, events organisation, and communicative roles. She also volunteers for an international solidarity network in the field of violence against women. Francesca holds an M.A. in Gender Studies from the School of Oriental and African Studies, University of London, and an M.A. in International Relations from the University of Bologna.

Joumana Seif was born in 1970 in Damascus, she holds a Law Degree and she is a Human Rights Activist. She is a representative of the Syrian Women Network in the Civil Society Support Rooms on the Margin of the Geneva Talks. She was elected member of the Follow-up Committee – Syrian Women's Initiative for Peace and Democracy under the auspices of the United Nations (Women's Bureau). She is Head of the Legal Committee in the Syrian Women's Network. She is a member of the Syrian Feminist Lobby which is an independent, non-party, political lobby group committed to equal participation of women and men in all political decision making processes concerning the future of Syria at all levels.

Massimiliano Trentin is Assistant Professor of History and IR of the Middle East at the Department of Political and Social Sciences, Alma Mater Studiorum, University of Bologna, Italy. He works on the International History of the Middle East and North Africa with a special focus on the interplay between diplomacy, economics, and patterns of development. His Ph.D. thesis, *Which kind of modernity for Syria? The construction of the Ba'thist regime under the shadow of the Berlin Wall* (University of Florence, 2008), dealt with the influence of economic and institutional development models of East and West Germany on Syria in the sixties and early seventies of the 20th century. His monograph, *Engineers of Modern Development: East German Experts in Ba'thist Syria, 1965-1972* (Cleup, 2010) and later editions, like *The Middle East and the Cold War. Between Security and Development* (Cambridge Scholars Publishing, 2012) and *La Guerra Fredda tedesca in Siria* (Cleup, 2015), focus on the critical conjuncture between Cold War interventions and patterns of development in the postcolonial Middle East. He currently works on the history of economic development in the Middle East and North Africa during the 'long' seventies and eighties and the influence of international economic organizations (World Bank, International Monetary Fund and UN Agencies) as a part of an international project on the history of energy in the 20th century.

Acknowledgements

The International Conference was jointly organized by

Center for Gender Studies of the University of Padova (CIRSG)

CENTRO
INTERDIPARTIMENTALE
DI RICERCA E
STUDI DI GENERE

Euromed Feminist Initiative (IFE-EFI)

IFE - EFI

The Center for Gender Studies of the University of Padova (CIRSG) is an interdepartmental entity operating to promote scientific and intellectual exchanges around gender issues and to disseminate a gender perspective within and across disciplines, with a focus on local situations and an international outlook. See: http://cirsg.unipd.it.

Euromed Feminist Initiative (IFE-EFI) is a policy network of women's rights organizations from the two shores of the Mediterranean that provides expertise on gender equality and women's rights as full parts of democracy and citizenship. Our headquarters are in Paris and our regional office is in Amman. See: www.efi-ife.org.

in collaboration with Next Generation Global Studies, University of Padova

Next Generation
Global Studies
www.nextgenerationglobalstudies.eu

with the Support of the European Commission External Action Service (EEAS) and the Swedish International Development Cooperation Agency Agency (project "Supporting the transition towards democracy in Syria through preparing for an engendered constitution building process").

SWEDEN

The contents of this document are the sole responsibility of the writers and can under no circumstances be regarded as reflecting the position of the European Union or Sweden.

List of acronyms

CEDAW: Convention on the Elimination of All Forms of Discrimination against Women

CIRSG: Interdepartmental Center for Gender Studies (University of Padova)

CSOs: Civil Society Organizations

CSTF: Cross Sector Task Force

CSWD: Coalition of Syrian Women for Democracy

ECC: Equal Citizenship Center

ECHR: European Court of Human Rights

EEAS: External Action Service of the European Commission

ESCWA: United National Economic Commission for Western Asia

EU: European Union

FSA: Free Syrian Army

GBV: Gender Based Violence

GR: General Recommendation

HIV: Human Immunodeficiency Virus

IACHR: Inter-American Commission on Human Rights

ICTJ: International Center for Transitional Justice

IFE-EFI: Initiative Féministe Euromed - Euromed Feminist Initiative

IOM: International Organization for Migration

IS: Islamic State

ISIS: Islamic State of Iraq and Syria

MENA: Middle East and North Africa

NAP: National Action Plan

NATO: North Atlantic Treaty Organization

NDF: National Defence Forces

NGGS: Next Generation Global Studies (University of Padova)

NGOs: Non Governmental Organizations

SAR: Syrian Arab Republic

SCPR: Syrian Center for Policy Research

SDF: Syrian Democratic Forces

SFL: Syrian Feminist Lobby

SPGI: Department of politics Law and International Studies (University of Padova)

SSR: Security Sector Reform

SWIPD: Syrian Women's Initiative for Peace and Democracy

SWN: Syrian Women Network

TFEU: Treaty on the Functioning of the European Union

TRC: Truth and Reconciliation Commission

UDHR: Universal Declaration of Human Rights

UN: United Nations

UNDP: United Nations Development Program

UNFPA: United Nations Population Fund

UNHCR: United Nations High Commissioner for Refugees

UNHRC: United Nations Human Rights Commission

UNOCHA: United Nations Office for the Coordination of Humanitarian Affairs

UNSCR: United Nations Security Council Resolution

VAW: Violence Against Women

WAB: Women's Advisory Board

WCW: World Conference on Women

WPS: Women, Peace, and Security

WMD: Weapons of Mass Destruction

Note from the editors

Claudia Padovani[1] and Francesca Helm[2]

On October 3rd, 2016, the University of Padova hosted an international conference entitled 'Rethinking the transition process in Syria: Constitution, participation, and gender equality'.

The event was the result of a joint collaboration between the Interdepartmental Center for Gender Studies (CIRSG) of the University of Padova and Euromed Feminist Initiative (IFE-EFI) in the context of a three year project called 'Supporting the transition towards democracy in Syria through preparing for an engendered constitution building process'. This was funded by the External Action Service of the European Commission and the Swedish government, and carried out by IFE-EFI. Support in the organization of the conference also came from the University of Padova's research group, Next Generation Global Studies (NGGS).

The event featured some of the most relevant voices that have been struggling for peace and gender equality in the Syrian context over the past years, and the aim of the conference was to investigate the key role of women in the Syrian transitional process, in view of promoting gender justice and social change in the perspective of a solution to the conflict that has affected the country since 2011.

Within this frame, the conference addressed questions such as: how should women's demands and voices be placed at the forefront of the negotiating tables, in order to secure women's fundamental rights and inclusive citizenship? How is it possible to envision drafting constitutional processes that acknowledge and include gender concerns? Under what conditions are such processes likely

1. Interdepartmental Center for Gender Studies (CIRSG), University of Padova, Padova, Italy; claudia.padovani@unipd.it

2. Next Generation Global Studies (NGGS), University of Padova, Padova, Italy; francesca.helm@unipd.it

How to cite: Padovani, C., & Helm, F. (2018). Note from the editors. In C. Padovani & F. Helm (Eds), *Rethinking the transition process in Syria: constitution, participation and gender equality* (pp. 1-10). Research-publishing.net. https://doi.org/10.14705/rpnet.2018.21.752

to develop in Syria's future, and what will women's roles be in the political transition?

Through a combination of academic reflection and advocacy expertise, historical and geo-political perspectives were presented, practical experiences from within the Syrian territory shared and discussed, and concrete proposals for gender aware transition processes to peace were introduced.

The conference was opened by the University of Padova Rector's delegate for working and studying conditions, Renzo Guolo. Then introductory remarks, setting the tone for the discussion, were offered by the Director of the CIRSG, Claudia Padovani, and by the Project Coordinator of IFE-EFI, Francesca Rondina. Three thematic sessions followed, respectively chaired by Paolo de Stefani (Center for Human Rights, University of Padova), Annalisa Oboe (University of Padova Rector's delegate for society, culture, and gender issues) and Francesca Rondina (IFE-EFI), with Alisa del Re (University of Padova) acting as discussant in the last session.

1.   About this volume

The present volume features most of the presentations made at the conference, in the diverse, direct, and lively styles – academic, advocacy, self-reflective – in which interventions were made. We edited all chapters so that this collection reflects the structure of the conference, as well as the productive collaboration between the University of Padova and IFE-EFI. Reflections and comments were made in 2016, over a year before this publication went to press, yet we feel the unprecedented character of this conversation – where the Syrian reality is critically investigated through women's eyes – make it still highly valuable for all interested actors, particularly in view of future developments in the country and the whole region. Clearly, we make no claim of encompassing the diverse views of the many women's realities and beliefs within the highly complex Syrian context, but only of those that have emerged within this important project.

The first part of the volume – entitled *Transitional justice from a gender-sensitive perspective: CEDAW and UN Resolution 1325* – is devoted to a critical discussion of the relevance of the Security Council Resolution 1325 and provisions that followed, according to which women should be actively engaged as central actors and decision-makers in mediation and peace-making processes, and in post-conflict developments. In reality, during conflicts as well as in processes of transition to peace, women's rights risk being bracketed; their concerns are not perceived as priority issues within scenarios of hardship, disorder, and widespread violence: a situation that ends up jeopardizing any effort in creating conditions for sustainable and lasting peace.

Lilian Halls French highlights the role of international advocacy networks to promote women's leading roles in peace processes, as IFE-EFI has done in Iraq, by supporting the adoption of a national action plan; an experience that may well inform future developments in Syria.

Lama Kannout, Coordinator of the Studies Committee of the Syrian Feminist Lobby (SFL), provides evidence from the ground, through the powerful voice of a Syrian woman who is directly involved in and affected by many of the processes described in this volume. Kannout gives examples of how the situation of many Syrian women is linked to the domestic laws, including the 2012 Syrian constitution, which discriminate against women, often through omissions (it contains no article prohibiting discrimination or violence against women) and the language used. Linking the local and international dimensions, Kannout also denounces the shortcomings in women's participation in the official peace negotiations.

Two scholarly contributions follow, providing legal insights and critical accounts.

Paola Degani focuses on women's experiences in humanitarian crises and on the actual impact of UN Security Council Resolutions, while stressing the importance of acknowledging the ordinary dimension of women's discrimination and subordination in order to explain the intersection of women's everyday life and their increased vulnerability in conflict and emergencies, as well as the several links between violence and inequality.

Sara Pennicino explores the relations between transitional justice and constitutionalism, paying particular attention to the issue of gender equality in constitution making. Examples from South Africa, Rwanda, former Yugoslavia, Tunisia, and Kosovo, as well as Syria, make a number of issues emerge as problematic nodes, including accountability of state and non-state actors, the international dimension of transitional justice, and the role of NGOs, as well as the specificities of local contexts for the delivery of justice.

The second part focuses on *The role of women in the Syrian uprising and in the political transitional process* and helps to clarify how relevant women and women's networks have been in the Syrian uprising from the very beginning; how crucial their role has been over the years to the survival of families and communities facing the conflict, inside and outside the country, and how fundamental it would be to properly acknowledge this role in current negotiations and forthcoming transition processes.

Providing the context to the following testimonies, **Massimiliano Trentin** offers a general, detailed, overview of the Syrian conflict from a historical, political perspective. His contribution sheds light on the main events in the transformation of what was a political conflict in 2011 into a full-scale war until late 2016. He identifies the main features of the political regimes that developed alongside the conflict, starting with the government 'regime' in Damascus and the fragmented opposition consisting of groups with different sources of political legitimacy who shared only a common stance against the regime, the international alliances they made, and then the different sets of government that have developed during the war in various regions of Syria.

Annalisa Oboe offers a vivid perspective of how women's experiences are constrained between empowerment and disempowerment in uprisings and revolutions. Making reference to the historical moment of the South African Truth and Reconciliation Commission, she brings testimony of how women may take up positions of responsibility and leadership in 'exceptional times'. However, she also points out that this offers no guarantee that those roles will be acknowledged once the revolutionary moment has passed, and that normalization comes with 'old style' silencing and marginalization.

Joumana Seif and **Mariam Jalabi**, both members of the Syrian Women's Network, a non-profit and independent network established in May 2013, speak from the standpoint of women in their engagement for social change and gender equality in Syria.

Joumana Seif opens her remarks asking if it is possible to obtain women's and human rights under a dictatorial regime; a question that had been raised among activists, in private and confidential forums, many years before the outbreak of the Syrian revolution, in which Syrian women had the main role from the very beginning. Hers is a lively account of women's initiatives since the revolution times, first within Syria and then – once the situation became too dangerous and many of them were forced to flee the country – by creating transnational networks of solidarity. It invites full appreciation of the many voices that have been, and still are, all too often marginalized, and yet keep trying to influence the official peace process at all levels. Seif concludes by listing a number of conditions – still relevant though the situation on the ground has changed profoundly over the past months – to be met in order to reach peace with justice.

Mariam Jalabi follows suit and stresses that to achieve gender equality in a future Syria, women would need to coordinate at every level of decision-making and contribute to establishing a constitution that institutionalizes a political space in which the equal rights and responsibilities of all Syrian men and women are protected and respected. The risk of women's voices going unheard remains high, including in international negotiations where Syrian women are often expected to espouse apolitical positions in favor of peace, while their acting and being inherently political is denied; hence Jalabi's call for strengthening women's political participation – internationally and locally – and for enshrining gender parity in the foundation of any political solution to the conflict and throughout the process of rebuilding.

The third part of the volume, *Launching the ABC for a gender sensitive constitution*, introduces an inspiring and challenging tool: an ABC guide – promoted by IFE-EFI and written by Sylvia Suteu (University College of London) and Ibrahim Draji (University of Damascus) – that includes theoretical background, normative references, and concrete suggestions towards drafting gender sensitive constitutions.

Co-author of the ABC guide **Ibrahim Draji** highlights states' responsibilities and obligations to engender their constitutions on the basis of international instruments mandating gender equality and non-discrimination, which call on states to implement such treaties and incorporate them into their national legislation. Draji introduces the content of 'democratic gender sensitive constitutions' which, amongst other aspects, ensures substantive gender equality both in theory and practice, prohibits discrimination, and pays attention to how provisions of the constitution impact on gender. Providing several examples, he also discusses the basic principles that are of special importance for women's rights, such as freedom, non-discrimination, separation of powers, and secularism.

Looking at the 'implementation problem', **Francesco Biagi** contributes a critical reflection on the potential for application of the gender equality principle in constitutional developments across the MENA region where, from Morocco to Egypt and Tunisia, constitutional reforms adopted following the Arab uprisings have significantly strengthened the provisions on women's rights. His central concerns are the main factors that may support or constrain the crucial process of constitutional implementation: discussing the nature of the constitution, the role played by the constitutional courts, limitation clauses, international treaties and conventions on human rights, women's representation in elected institutions, and the social, cultural, and religious context. Biagi calls our attention to how the implementation of 'superior laws' could concretely foster gender equality.

Finally, **Maya Alrahabi**, General Coordinator of the Coalition of Syrian Women for Democracy, recalls the realities of the Syrian conflict over the past years, and the suffering of women and feminist activists in that context: arrested and tortured, some of them killed. She denounces the international patriarchal order that legalizes wars, and highlights the ways in which women advocates have attempted to foster conflict resolution, from the local and national, to the supranational level. Criticizing the tendency in the international community for the standardization of the role of women as victims of wars seeking peace, she argues for a sustainable just peace which will only be achieved by striking a balance between forgiveness and accountability, setting up institutional mechanisms, and realizing a specific set of principles to be enshrined in a gender-responsive constitution.

Together, these chapters make a strong argument in support of UN Resolution 1325 and its follow ups: they call for explicit commitments from all parties to include women's voices, knowledge, and determination in designing and building a future for Syria. At the same time, they illustrate the fact that solutions to the Syrian conflict, and to engendering the transition to peace, are neither simple nor one-track, as shown by a number of transversal concerns that run through the collection. These include: the contradiction between the central roles played by women at the outburst of the revolution and the gradual side-lining, whereby women found themselves within a war zone dominated by men, and yet struggling to continue their work and establishing safe spaces for women and children; there is the need for National Action Plans (NAPs), institutionalized mechanisms for political inclusion, and recognition of fundamental principles of gender equality at the highest level of the juridical system, but also the large and persistent gaps between the adoption of formal documents and the implementation of principles and programs. Also considered by the contributors are the multifaceted responsibilities of governments, on the one hand, who should be held accountable for policies and the implementation of legal provisions, and of the international community, on the other, that has yet to fully acknowledge the crucial contribution of women towards a lasting peace and to set up adequate mechanisms for a meaningful inclusion of women in the Syrian peace processes.

Speakers who contributed their knowledge and understanding came from both academia and civic organizations and networks, in the attempt to create a space for 'action-focused intellectual exchange': a space to share knowledges and learn from different perspectives and expertise.

In particular, facing the risk that in current and future peace negotiation and post-conflict developments women are once again side-lined, both by the international community and domestically, the accounts offered in this collection through Syrian women's own voices should be highly valued. They reflect the spirit and respond to the goals of the UN Resolution 1325 (2000) that calls for women to be listened to, and included as actors in full right to all phases of peace negotiations and beyond.

The fourth part of the volume, *Testimonies by civil society organizations and Syrian lawyers' internships at the CIRSG and SPGI*, also reports short interventions made on the occasion of a public session that was held in the evening of October 3rd, 2016, at Teatro Ruzante, with the participation of **Massimiliano Fanni Canelles** (President of the Auxilia foundation) and **Giulia D'Odorico** (Trama di Terre, Imola). Finally, two short pieces are included, by young lawyers **Roula Baghdadi** and **Yousef Razouk**, who were visiting scholars at the University of Padova in the first half of the same year.

We believe that listening to all those voices, and relating them to the insights coming from academia, is crucial for scholars and interested observers, as well as for the international community and decision-makers who have direct responsibility for putting an end to the gross violation of human rights in the region. We trust the inspiring conversation accounted for in this volume will constitute a meaningful contribution towards a much needed understanding of the crucial role women should play, as social and political actors, in peace-building processes and in the long struggle for human and women's rights in Syria and across the Middle East.

2. Synthetic timeline of the Syrian peace process

Several of the contributions to this collection mention specific moments of the Syrian peace process, a set of initiatives to resolve the Syrian Civil War which started in 2011. Here we provide a synthetic timeline of events related to this process.

The Syrian peace process has been moderated by several institutions and forces: the United Nations (UN) and its Special Envoys on Syria, the Arab League, Russia, and Western Powers. The negotiating parties are typically representatives of the Syrian Ba'athist government and Syrian opposition forces, whose composition has changed over time according to the differentiated phases of the armed conflict. Notably, Kurdish forces have been precluded from most of the negotiation frameworks; whereas radical islamist forces, and the organization of the islamic state (ISIS/ISIL) have refused to engage in contacts on peaceful resolution to the conflict.

The attempts to find a solution to the Syrian conflict began in late 2011, when the Arab League launched two initiatives, without much success. Russia in January 2012 and in November 2013 suggested talks in Moscow between the Syrian government and the opposition.

In March-June 2012, the UN and the Arab League coordinated a new plan, led by Kofi Annan, Joint Special Envoy for the United Nations and the Arab League, called Geneva I.

In January and February 2014, the Geneva II Conference on Syria took place, organized by Lakhdar Brahimi, the new UN Special Envoy to Syria. In July 2014, Staffan de Mistura was appointed Special Envoy for Syria.

On October 30th 2015, intergovernmental talks started in Vienna involving officials from the US, the EU, Russia, China, and various regional actors such as Saudi Arabia, Egypt, Turkey, and, for the first time, Iran. In December of the same year, the UN Security Council adopted Resolution 2254, indicating bases for the political transition in Syria.

Attempts for a Geneva III were made by UN Envoy de Mistura in late January 2016, but were suspended after a few days.

In early February 2016, the UN Special Envoy for Syria announced the appointment of a Women's Advisory Board (WAB). Composed of twelve women from the different parties to the conflict, the WAB is politically unaffiliated. It does not participate in the negotiations, but advises the UN mediator on all proceedings. Criticism of the lack of transparency in member selection led to the Syrian Women's Network to withdraw from the WAB.

The Geneva peace process continued between the Syrian government and the Syrian opposition under the auspices of the UN: Geneva IV in April 2016, Geneva V in February 2017, Geneva VI in May 2017, and Geneva VII in July 2017.

Peace talks to stop the armed clashes between the Syrian government and opposition forces, now including armed rebel leaders too, were led by Russia in Astana, Kazakhstan, together with Turkey and Iran in the course of 2017.

Opening speech expressed
at the international conference

Claudia Padovani[1]

"Distinguished guests, Euromed Feminist Initiative (IFE-EFI) members, dear students, colleagues, I speak today as the Director of the Center for Gender Studies at the University of Padova that is co-hosting this event together with IFE-EFI.

I feel it is an extremely meaningful event that we are hosting today: in addressing the complex and tragic reality of the Syrian conflict, this conference aims at investigating one specific aspect which is all too often left aside in policy debates and remains invisible in media accounts of conflict areas and struggles for peace and democracy, that is: the key role of women in conflict and transitional processes – and in the Syrian context in particular – in order to promote gender justice and social change within and across communities in the Middle Eastern region.

This occasion stems out of a recent collaboration our center had with IFE-EFI. In the context of a project they are conducting with the support of the European Union in early 2016 for a period of five months, we hosted two young Syrian lawyers in Padova. They came to meet with us at the Center for Gender Studies and got involved in our activities at the Department of Law, Politics, and International Studies. They took courses and participated in our scientific initiatives and they met our students and engaged with local civic organizations. Roula Baghdadi and Yousef Razouk, through sharing their experiences and visions, certainly enriched our perspective on the complexities that characterize the Syrian context today, and the Middle East more generally.

---

1. Director, Interdepartmental Center for Gender Studies, University of Padova, Padova, Italy; claudia.padovani@unipd.it

How to cite: Padovani, C. (2018). Opening speech expressed at the international conference. In C. Padovani & F. Helm (Eds), *Rethinking the transition process in Syria: constitution, participation and gender equality* (pp. 11-14). Research-publishing.net. https://doi.org/10.14705/rpnet.2018.21.753

At some point, we felt it would have been crucial to create an opportunity to bring some of this understanding to a broader audience in the premises of a university that – as a place of knowledge production and sharing – has a mandate to promote a culture based on universal values of human rights, peace, environmental protection, and international solidarity. So we started, together with IFE-EFI, to plan for this international event.

We decided the focus of the discussion would be on how to better understand the role and the contribution of women in peace processes, and what are the challenges they face in their efforts to promote and protect human and women's rights in ongoing conflicts and in constitution building, as well as in transition and post-conflict situations.

Indeed, it is crucial to make clear that gender gaps – in both peace talks and transitional phases, as well as before and beyond emergency situations – are a persistent and universal challenge to national as well as international solidarity: as issues of gender exclusion, women's marginalization, and stereotypes persist at all levels and across social and cultural backgrounds, feminist analyses can help understand the connection between daily experiences of gender-based discrimination and crisis situations, between 'ordinary' and 'extra-ordinary' forms of violence against women, such as those we have witnessed during the long years of the Syrian conflict.

By adopting this perspective, and looking at national conflicts and international developments through a gender lens, we also want to highlight the responsibility of the many actors and institutions that have a role to play when the challenges of gender equality and women's empowerment are immense and when a politics of recognition *and* political will would be core to take the formal principles of respect, dignity, and equality for women and men that are enshrined in international standards and constitutional laws to the more concrete level of actual implementation.

Historical, juridical, and geo-political perspectives will be presented today, and practical experiences from within the Syrian territory will be shared and discussed. Indeed, we need these diverse perspectives and disciplinary approaches to be brought to us so that we can all understand how norms evolve internationally, impact on national contexts, and learn from a dialog amongst different knowledges – those emerging from academia and those elaborated through political activities on the ground and transnationally – to try and make sense of the complexities of the current situation.

We have the privilege today of listening to some of the voices that have been struggling for gender equality and peace in the Syrian context over the past years: advocates and activists whom we normally do not hear about; actions and struggles that are seldom reported in the news, even when the news *is* about the violation of human and women's rights.

We shall have three sessions in our conference: one devoted to a better understanding of international juridical standards as critical tools for moving the gender equality agenda forward, in conflict and post-conflict situations; a second one focusing on how women's rights organizations in Syria support women's claims to play a key role in the transition towards democracy and regime change; and a third session where an *ABC for a Gender Sensitive Constitution*, produced by IFE-EFI, will be introduced and commented upon.

There is also a 'civil society dialog' organized in the evening. That session gathers civil society organizations from Syria and Italy to address the Syrian conflict and its tragic consequences with a gender lens. The aim is to discuss the impact of the conflict on women, girls, and children; as well as to address the implications on the refugee issues that are at the core of Italian and European democratic crises nowadays.

As I said, we have worked in close collaboration with IFE-EFI to make this happen, and this has been a pleasure. But I would also like to thank all those who have contributed in different ways: our Syrian speakers, who have come a long way to tell their stories and expectations; our Italian colleagues, who have agreed to share their expertise; members of the Center for Gender Studies and staff at our Department, for continued organizational support; our hosts in this amazing space; our video-makers; and our translators.

Finally, I would like to take the opportunity to remind everyone that the Center for Gender Studies is part of an evolving network of similar centers across Italy, and is strengthening its connections with European and International realities engaged with the promotion of a culture of gender equality, from the local to the global level, within and beyond academia.

This broad network – as well as an internationally interested audience – will have access to the content of our conference thanks to a video recording that will be made available on our respective websites. The presentations will also be collected in a publication. In this manner, we aim to give continuity to the effort that is initiated today.

As we are daily confronted with the tragedy of conflicts and human and women's rights violations, we are also faced with the questions: how can we contribute to making women's struggles for peace known? How can *their* voices enter *our* communication channels, *our* research communities, and *our* educational activities?

We, at the Center for Gender Studies, wish today's event will contribute to making these spaces for dialog – and the collaborations through which they are made possible – part of our ongoing academic commitment and practice.

I wish you all a fruitful conference".

Opening remarks on the publication

Francesca Rondina[1]

This publication is the result of a fruitful cultural cooperation and shared vision on the Syrian human crisis between Euromed Feminist Initiative (IFE-EFI) and the University of Padova.

I would first like to thank Claudia Padovani from the Interdepartmental Center for Gender Studies of Padova University; Francesca Helm from the Next Generation Global Studies Group; the Department of Political Science, Law, and International Relations; the international service Servizio Accoglienza Ospiti Stranieri (SAOS); the university accommodation service (SASSA); Lucille Delbecchi; Tania Toffanin; Barbara Gollin; and all the people who were committed and dedicated to the organization of the internships and of this conference.

I was deeply honoured to be present at the Museum of the History of Medicine representing IFE-EFI. Founded in 2003, IFE-EFI is a network of women's rights organizations from the two shores of the Mediterranean and from Caucasus. It advocates for gender equality and women's universal human rights as inseparable from democracy building and citizenship, for political solutions to all conflicts, and for the people's right to self-determination. IFE-EFI headquarters are in Paris and our regional office is in Amman.

The conference aimed at sharing insights and facilitating discussions among academics, Syrian women's rights activists, students, and citizens on issues of deep importance that are at the core of IFE-EFI's projects in the Middle East and North African region, and of those of us working for women's empowerment and rights.

1. IFE-EFI Project Coordinator, Paris, France; rondinafrancesca@gmail.com

How to cite: Rondina, F. (2018). Opening remarks on the publication. In C. Padovani & F. Helm (Eds), *Rethinking the transition process in Syria: constitution, participation and gender equality* (pp. 15-17). Research-publishing.net. https://doi.org/10.14705/rpnet.2018.21.754

If some of you are still wondering why this gendered lens was adopted for the International Conference, there are three main reasons that reflect the topics of the sessions.

First, the implementation of the Convention on the Elimination of All Forms of Discrimination against Women (CEDAW) and path-breaking United Nations Security Council Resolution 1325 on women, peace, and security. These legal tools must be used together to broaden, strengthen, and operationalize gender equality in conflict, peace-building, and post-conflict reconstruction stressing the pivotal role women should play in all these phases. However, in order to transform the verb 'should play' into 'do play', a lot of work needs to be done. Only with women's full participation and representation in the political sphere at international, national, and local levels will women's human rights be secured, gender-based violence be tackled, and an inclusive democracy prospected.

Second, the exclusion of women from decision making processes. Although Syrian women have been at the forefront of the Syrian uprising from the beginning and have been playing crucial roles throughout its phases, roles that have shifted over time in response to the militarization and violence on the ground, they are systematically side-lined from political decision-making regarding the future of their country.

Third, the gender-sensitive constitution process: within the framework of a program co-funded by the European Union and the Swedish International Development Cooperation Agency, IFE-EFI and Syrian partners worked together towards a gender-sensitive constitution that combines the establishment of the rule of law, equality between women and men, and respect for human rights and dignity of both women and men alike. This work led to the publication of a handbook, ABC for a Gender-Sensitive Constitution[2].

So now is precisely the time for the challenge of the Syrian transition to be raised and dealt with through a gendered approach. I would therefore like to

---

2. Suteu, S., & Draji, I. (2015). ABC for a Gender Sensitive Constitution. Euromed Feminist Initiative IFE-EFI. https://www.efi-ife.org/sites/default/files/ABC%20for%20a%20Gender%20Sensitive%20Constitution.pdf

thank our Syrian contributors: Maya Alrhabi, Executive Director of Women's Studies Center and General Coordinator of the Coalition of Syrian Women for Democracy; Lama Kannout, Coordinator of the Studies Committee at the Syrian Feminist Lobby; and Joumana Seif, Head of the Legal Committee of the Syrian Women Network.

Thanks to all of you for participating in the Padova Conference and for your drive and involvement for Syrian women's rights both at grassroot and international levels.

Furthermore, Mariam Jalabi, member of the Syrian Women Network and Syrian Feminist Lobby based in New York, joined the Conference through Skype; and Ibrahim Draji, Professor in International Law at the University of Damascus, also participated remotely during the session on the ABC for a Gender Sensitive Constitution, which he co-authored with Dr Silvia Suteu, from the University College in London.

Through Syrian lawyers' first-hand experiences and angles, we brought into light the resilience and resourcefulness of women who are usually depicted only as 'vulnerable women in need of protection' by dominant patriarchal discourses in the mainstream coverage of the Syrian conflict. If Europe desires a political solution for Syria, a country that is approaching its seventh year of war, national unity, inclusive democracy, human rights, and lasting peace, then women's voices need to be heard, too.

Finally, this conference contributed to engendering a multi-faceted view of the current Syrian context and its dramatic consequences and will hopefully have an impact on attitudes towards refugees based on human dignity, human security, protection of asylum seekers, and solidarity. I strongly believe that this initiative can pave the way for further academic, social, and cultural cooperation between Syria and Italy.

Section 1.

Transitional justice from a gender-sensitive perspective: CEDAW and UN Resolution 1325

This session investigates the protection of women during armed conflict and their participation in peace and security decision-making. Two sets of standards – UN Security Council Resolution 1325 on women, peace, and security (UNSCR 1325), and the Convention on the Elimination of All Forms of Discrimination against Women (CEDAW) – are critical tools for moving the gender equality agenda forward in conflict and post-conflicts contexts; but it is also crucial to understand the limits and challenges to their implementation and the follow up provisions and mechanisms that have been elaborated in relation to specific situations in recent years.

Peace and security for whom?

Lilian Halls French[1]

The Euromed Feminist Initiative (IFE-EFI)[2] is a network that brings together women's rights organisations from Europe, Maghreb, and Middle East. All of them have the same belief that feminism is a driving force behind the transformations that our societies urgently need, all over the world. I would like to highlight here some of IFE-EFI's analyses on peace and security. Let me first remind everyone that one of the objectives of this conference is to continue supporting the advocacy work of the Syrian women's rights activists and to provide them expanded space to discuss and advocate for their demands. IFE-EFI has been working with them for several years, contributing to the efforts of preparing a democratic future for Syria inclusive of women's rights and gender equality. The University of Padova has been associated to this work by welcoming two young lawyers for a five-month internship and for both sides, this experience was a very fruitful one!

Peace and security are among the major issues that frame the action of our network, and United Nations Security Council Resolution (UNSCR) 1325[3] is one of the major tools we use to preserve women's rights rights and security, together with other international and regional statements and resolutions, above all the Convention on the Elimination of All Forms of Discrimination against Women (CEDAW). The gender gap in both peace and transitional phases is a persistent and universal challenge. Thus, women's struggle for political and social change needs strong international solidarity to expose both the prevalence of militaristic

---

1. Co-president, Euromed Feminist Initiative, Paris, France; lilian.hallsfrench@efi-ife.org

2. http://www.efi-ife.org/

3. https://goo.gl/5S9IUn

How to cite this chapter: Halls French, L. (2018). Peace and security for whom? In C. Padovani & F. Helm (Eds), *Rethinking the transition process in Syria: constitution, participation and gender equality* (pp. 21-27). Research-publishing.net. https://doi.org/10.14705/rpnet.2018.21.755

values, and male-dominated cultures and norms that lead to limited space and access for women's political and social role and influence.

Today, we are globally confronted with an unprecedented wave of reactionary political movements and religious fundamentalisms that threaten people's lives and deny their rights to freedom, social justice, and peace. We are facing the rise of bloody conflicts, the pursuit of repressive regimes, and occupying forces that kill and imprison people to stifle all voices defending human rights. Women's rights, as universal human rights, are particularly targeted. That's why there are urgent steps to lay the foundation for political solutions to the conflicts in which women play an equal and significant leading role.

As feminists, we are pacifists and used to questioning the traditional approach of peace and security, and we strive to uncover the emptiness of dominant discourses based on domination, control over the other, military action, and destruction. We strive to unveil the continuum of violence against women during peace and war and to get from the States the integration of this structural violence as part of their security policies. We stress that human security truly merits its name only if it includes the two components of Humanity. In times of crises and conflicts, the issue of gender equality is more than ever pushed at the background of the public debate, while it should be the opposite.

Why is there such a persistent gender gap in the planning of both peace and transitional processes that take societies out of conflicts and dictatorships in spite of the role played by women? Peace processes are built upon a combination of different factors.

The first obstacle is related to the specific patriarchal legacy of societies and universal traditional patriarchal values. This combination results in different forms of discrimination against women after conflicts are over and during the political transitions that follow. Therefore, women's active participation for social change and for keeping the community going during violent conflicts does not translate into their proportional participation in formal peace processes and decision making under the following transitional period.

The debate on women's participation in decision-making processes often leads to the same questions about 'the difference that women would make'. For us, this participation is not a matter of 'plus' or efficiency, on which difference women would make, but a basic matter of social justice. In other words, the presence of women is not measurable in terms of impact, but it is a measure of democracy. This means that all decision-making processes, peace processes among them, should include equal representation and participation of women.

The second is related to the power structures that maintain women in a subordinated position all over the world. As we know, one of their bases is militarism that sustains and strengthens the supremacy of military values on culture, identity, and norms of society on public institutions and policies. Militarist culture is a major barrier to the presence of women in decision making in the field of security.

The third is the strength of stereotypes about the myth of a feminine identity characterized by a so-called women's lack of taste and incapacity to deal with power or to manage difficult negotiations. This 'femininity' has always been used to exclude women from history. Our network, IFE-EFI, acts with all the components of the democratic movement for the development, in the whole Euromed region, of political tools to eradicate these stereotypes – as early as at school – and to denounce the increasing intrusion of religions in the public sphere that contribute to consolidating them.

The last obstacle is linked to the nature of peace negotiations: as political processes, they are male-shaped in their composition, functioning, language, and history. Women are welcomed to intervene on 'women's issues', supposed to be 'their' specific issues, and not issues related to half of humanity.

How to face all these obstacles? The first necessity is the implementation by the States of actions counteracting dominant discourses on militarism that penalize fundamental women's rights in the name of national security. Besides, together with all components of the feminist movement, we have to convince the democratic political and associative movement of the urgency to take into account feminist analyses as it is the only way to build a democratic world.

Last and not least, it is crucial to promote the UNSC Resolution 1325 and work for its implementation. This resolution, adopted in 2000, reaffirms the important role of women in the prevention and resolution of conflicts, peace negotiations, peace building, peace keeping, and in post-conflict reconstruction. It stresses the importance of equal participation and full involvement of women in the maintenance and promotion of peace and security. It urges all actors to increase this participation and incorporates gender perspectives in all United Nations (UN) peace and security strategies. It also calls on all parties of the conflicts to take special measures to protect women and girls from gender-based violence, particularly rape and sexual abuse in situations of armed conflict. This resolution provides a number of important operational mandates, with implications for Member States and entities of the UN system.

For the first time, women are not only approached as 'victims' or as a 'vulnerable group' by the UN Security Council. Resolution 1325 focuses on women as agents in their own right in situations of conflict and post-conflict. It recognizes the unbalanced and gender-specific impact of conflicts on women, but also highlights the very limited role of women in the prevention and resolution of conflicts and in peace-building and post-conflict reconstruction. In Article 1, it calls for the "increased representation of women at all decision-making levels in [...] prevention, management, and resolution of conflicts". In Article 8, it requires all participants to the negotiation and implementation of peace agreements to "adopt a gender perspective".

Even if three other Resolutions have also been adopted after 1325 to preserve women's rights in conflict situations – UNSCR 1820, 1888 and 1890 – UNSCR 1325 is important because it is mandatory for all member states. As such, it is a precious tool in the hands of civil society to make governments accountable.

In this year of the 16th anniversary of the Resolution, what has been achieved? The reports about sexual violence in conflict zones and the persistent under-representation of women in peace negotiations and post-conflict governance highlight the huge gap between the adoption of the resolution and its implementation. As early as 2004, the UN called on Member States to develop National Action Plans as the most effective way to fill this gap. As the Resolution was written in general terms concerning women's needs in all conflict and post-conflict areas, its implementation needs national plans with specific, measurable, and time-limited objectives. Furthermore, the change of women's situation "requires specific actions and policies, accountability mechanisms for the different ministries and respective authorities, a concrete allocated budget, transparency, and [therefore] evaluation and monitoring reporting mechanisms"[4].

With the support of the Norwegian Embassy, IFE-EFI initiated, supported, and facilitated the development of the National Action Plan (NAP) for the implementation of the UNSCR 1325 in Iraq 2012-2014. The plan was adopted in 2014.

The main objectives[5] of this project were through the plan to:

- increase the effective and proportional participation of women in decision-making positions on local and national levels in all reconciliation committees and peace-building negotiations;

- increase quotas as an affirmative action on all levels: executive, legislative, and judiciary and in the local communities to allow women to play their role in decision making;

- harmonize national legislation with international standards and mechanisms for women's human rights, including UNSCR 1325, annul laws which violate women rights, and promulgate/enact legislations that protect and promote them;

---

4. http://www.equalpowerlastingpeace.org/tag/national-action-plan/

5. http://www.peacewomen.org/assets/image/iraq_nap.pdf?

- strengthen women's agency through right-based approaches;

- integrate and mainstream gender in in all policies and processes related to conflict prevention, conflict resolution, and peace-building in Iraq.

Via this project, Iraq has become the first country in the Middle East and North Africa (MENA) region to have such a plan. It was adopted in 2014. Its development was carried out by a Cross Sector Task Force (CSTF) composed of State actors, representatives from relevant ministries, members of parliament, judiciary courts, and the 'INAP 1325 Initiative' – an informal network of women's rights organizations and networks in the civil society – from Iraq and Kurdistan.

IFE-EFI is now supporting the phase of implementation that can also have an impact on regional peace and stability. Exchanges have already taken place with Syrian activists on the Iraqi experience and the lessons learned from this process. The last report provides an overview of the collective and individual efforts of Iraqi ministries, security institutions, and civil society in implementing the plan in a very challenging context. Analysing the achievements, as well as the challenges and the gaps in the implementation will help the CSTF in addressing them during the development of the second national plan.

The key provisions of the resolution, captured by three P's (protection of human rights of women and girls during times of conflict, prevention of sexual and gender-based violence, and equal participation of women in peace building and reconstruction), are addressed by the Iraqi National Action Plan. A fourth pillar related to economic empowerment was also integrated, responding to the actual needs of women. Legal actions have also been elaborated in order to enable the implementation of the resolution. Approaching these issues in a comprehensive manner, the national plan has thus become an important tool to enhance the implementation of measures guaranteeing an increased level of security and participation of women in rebuilding society.

The added value of this national plan is its collaborative and consultative process which ensured broad ownership. Furthermore, the common work on its development and implementation provided space for all involved to responsibly enhance skills and increase capacities in the field of women's rights as well as for understanding the interconnected nature of women's meaningful participation in decision making and building peace and security.

Most of all, we hope that this work has contributed to an improved situation for women on the ground, who are the real actors for change.

As stated above, to face the immensity of the present challenges, feminist perspectives must be shared and adopted by the democratic movement. In parallel, immediate steps must be taken by all States to stop the bloodshed, to act for global demilitarization, and the end of occupation. Without this, no advancement of any rights can be achieved, as militarism and sacrifice of rights, in particular women's rights, in the name of national security, will prevail. It is our common responsibility, researchers and women's rights activists together, to intensify our efforts in order to reach our common goal: a peaceful and secure world, where security will equally benefit women and men and not only half of humanity.

2 Resolution 1325: advantages and disadvantages[1]

Lama Kannout[2]

When they launched their revolution in 2011 to ask for freedom, the Syrian men and women knew that the regime would treat them with utmost violence, as history is full of horror stories from the eighties in Hama. However, the violence would not have reached this level of savagery in the face of the communities that rebelled peacefully had it not been for the fact that the regime was reassured that it would be safe from accountability and safe from sanctions. The Security Council was divided and remained incapable of referring the Syrian file to the International Criminal Court due to a double veto from Russia and China. The Russian-American deal (resolution 2118 dated September 27th, 2013) that stated that the regime was to submit its chemical weapons system, after it had perpetrated the chemical massacre of Eastern Gota in the Damascus countryside, was a signal to allow it to kill the Syrians using any other weapons, including exploding barrels, napalm, and prohibited weapons.

The regime skilfully implemented its logo 'Assad or we burn the country' or 'Assad forever', and it brought in fanatic invaders (Afghans, Iraqis, Iranians, and Lebanese) that stood on the hills of the cities whose besieged populations were coerced to leave, and it handed over the sovereignty of the country to whomever would ensure the perennity of its rule. In return, the enemies of freedom and democracy – supported by countries from the region with the force of weapons and fatwas – pursued the plan of oppression and destruction as Syria turned into an offering on the altar of freedom, eaten up by the game of interests and nations.

1. These arguments were further discussed in the author's book (Kannout, 2017).

2. Syrian Feminist Lobby, Coordinator of the Studies Committee, Beirut, Lebanon; lamakannout@gmail.com

How to cite this chapter: Kannout, L. (2018). Resolution 1325: advantages and disadvantages. In C. Padovani & F. Helm (Eds), *Rethinking the transition process in Syria: constitution, participation and gender equality* (pp. 29-38). Research-publishing.net. https://doi.org/10.14705/rpnet.2018.21.756

As regards the general situation and the specific situation of Syrian women, at the time of writing, the number of registered Syrian refugees exceeded 4.8 million, and 7.6 million are displaced in Syria – United Nations High Commissioner for Refugees (UNHCR, 2016) –, 45% of inhabitants had to leave their residences and some have had to do so more than once. "More than 145,000 Syrian refugee families in Egypt, Lebanon, Iraq, and Jordan – [one family out of four] – are headed by women struggling on their own to survive" (UNHCR, 2014); they also suffer from poverty, lack of aid, and difficulty in obtaining documentation. They have no skills for work, and if they do they face exploitation, sexual harassment, sexual attacks, or forced marriage. Furthermore, according to the discriminatory laws that are in place, they cannot circulate with their children, nor can they give them nationality or have custody of them. The number of school dropouts due to the conflict (UNICEF report 2015)[3] is 2.6 million Syrian boys and girls. Over 20% of Syrian schools have been destroyed and 20% of male and female teachers lost, and the general poverty level was estimated at 85.2% in 2015, the percentage of which living in extreme poverty reaching 69.3% (UNHCR, 2016). These people are incapable of ensuring their basic needs, be they nutritional or other.

1.   Constitutional discrimination

Syrian women have crumbled under legalized violence and discrimination for decades, both in the private and public spheres. There are many coercive laws against women – personal status laws, penal codes, nationality laws, and reservations on the Convention on the Elimination of all Forms of Discrimination Against Women (CEDAW). Article 3 of the 2012 constitution[4], in paragraphs 1, 2 and 4, states the following:

- Paragraph 1: "The religion of the President of the Republic is Islam". This paragraph is in line with paragraph four of article 84 that sets

---

3. www.unicef.org/about/annualreport/files/Syria_Arab_Republic_2015_COAR.pdf

4. http://ncro.sy/wp-content/uploads/2016/04/2012.pdf

conditions for the candidate to the presidency: "he is not to be married to a non Syrian woman", which means that women are deprived from their right of being in the position of President of the Republic.

- Paragraph 2: "Islamic jurisprudence shall be a major source of legislation". This means the enforcement of the most discriminatory and strict stipulations on women in the personal status laws, the penal code, nationality laws, labour laws, and the social insurance law, since this male dominated doctrine is based on the principles of guardianship and wardship, which go against the charter of human rights for women and men and international treaties.

- Paragraph 4: "The personal status of religious confessions shall be protected and respected". This is a consecration of sectarianism in society as it becomes part of the constitution, given that there are eight personal status laws[5] that consecrate discrimination against women and deprive them of their civil rights, giving control of their lives to religious instances.

The constitution does not include a definition of discrimination against women as stipulated by CEDAW, or an article that prohibits discrimination and violence against them, which has increased the harm done against women. Nor does it include a clear article that establishes the importance of international agreements in relation to national laws, which deprive women of legal opportunities to amend discriminatory laws based on the stipulations of these agreements. For instance, the personal status laws consecrate discrimination and violence against women through their content, language, and practice regarding issues related to marriage, divorce, custody, wardship, guardianship, movement, inheritance, and certification, along with the absence of equality between males and females

---

5. Comparative study: "Discrimination in the Personal Status Laws in Syria" authored by a group of female researchers, Edition Atar 2014. Personal status laws, general personal status law for Muslims, for Christian Orthodox, Armenian Orthodox, Catholics, Confessional Evangelical courts in Syria and Lebanon, and the book of legal rulings for personal status for the Jews, the special stipulations of the Druze confession included in article (307) of the general personal status law. The code of religious sects: issued by the French High Commissioner Lamartine according to the decision 60 LR of 1936 that established the sects that are recognized in Syria and that each have the right to adopt their own personal status laws.

regarding the minimum age for marriage, etc. Article 305 of the law stipulates that for all matters not mentioned in this law, the judge goes back to the most agreed upon text in the Hanafi School in the Kadri Pasha Law, meaning subjecting women to rules that are almost one hundred years old: "anything that is not mentioned in the text of this law is resolved as per the most widely recognized in the Hanafi School".

2. The political participation of women in the official negotiations

In Geneva 2, on January 22nd, 2014, two out of 15 members of the opposition delegation were women, along with two women in the regime's delegation. On December 9th, 2015, out of the 115 members of the opposition conference that was held in Riyadh, only ten were women. The conference led to the creation of a 'Supreme Commission for Negotiations' that included 32 persons including two women only. This body formed the negotiating delegation to Geneva III. It included three women out of 15 members. As for the regime's delegation, it included the participation of four women out of 15 members. It cannot be considered that the ratio of women in the regime's delegation is an indicator of democracy, as they do not express anything but the official discourse and they do not dare criticize the authorities; they are fierce in defending decisions that violate their rights. Their nomination was based on their allegiance to a regime of despotism and corruption.

On the level of the local councils[6] in the areas outside of the authority of the regime, women are almost absent and work in very hard conditions as they are systematically targeted with all the means of killing and starvation along with explosive barrel attacks and the use of prohibited weapons. On the other hand, they face the tyranny of Salafi armed groups, as for the areas of control of the regime their ratio is 3% (in the tenth electoral cycle, 2011) (Al Chaher, 2015). The Syrian

---

6. Definition of local councils and their goals can be found at http://www.etilaf.org.

Feminist Lobby[7] is concerned with the political participation of women and their right to the same level of access to decision making positions as men and the right to build their country, establish policies, and free it from tyranny in all its forms. It is fully aware of the importance of Resolution 1325. Thus, we have started – with the support of Euromed Feminist Initiative (IFE-EFI) – working on publishing an informational guide on how to draft a national plan for the resolution to achieve its objective. The guide includes recommendations such as:

- Providing knowledge to male and female Syrian decision makers, and to the office of the United Nations (UN) envoy to Syria and the influential countries in the Syrian file explaining the importance of having a national plan for Resolution 1325 and the priorities of women in three phases: the current/conflict phase, the transitional phase, and the phase of building the state.

- Providing advocacy material to the human rights defenders for men and women, and Civil Society Organizations (CSOs).

- Informing the countries of the region about the importance of Resolution 1325 and drafting national plans to implement it, as the countries hosting female Syrian refugees and the local organizations whether national, regional, or international that took part in the Syrian file did not include the concept and implementation of Resolution 1325 in their programs. The regime in Syria has not set contingency programs for the protection of women despite the horrendous conditions they live in. According to the speech delivered by Assad[8] in presence of a number of Sheikhs and Islam advocates in Damascus on April 23rd, 2014 where he called millions of Syrians 'terrorists', he meant the popular incubator of cities

---

7. The Syrian Feminist Lobby, an independent political lobby not affiliated to a party committed to equal participation of men and women in all political decision making processes in Syria and in all fields, the members of this lobby are convinced that democracy cannot be built without respect and full implementation of women's rights as part of the international human rights and the principles of full equality between men and women both in the private and public life. See: http://syrianfeministlobby.com/aside-post/

8. Assad in an encounter with the Oulemas (Islamic advocates and religious instances) where he describes hundreds of thousands of Syrians (with a social support, there is a relative, a neighbour or a friend) as terrorists. See: https://www.youtube.com/watch?v=_l0zcjPQv8Y

and villages that rebelled against him. Also, in one of his speeches on June 3rd, 2012[9], he said: "and I say to be accurate that the President is for all those who are under the umbrella of the state, constitution, and law or else I would be putting on the same level the traitor and the patriot, and the victim and the torturer, and the corrupt and the honest, and the destructor and the constructor", meaning that he is a president for his supporters and allegiants only. As for those who rebelled against him like the male or female activists and the defenders of human rights, they have been uprooted, detained, or forced into exile as they were called traitors, terrorists, and destructors.

- Informing the upcoming transitional ruling body according to Resolution 2254, Geneva I, about the importance of drafting a national plan for the resolution.

Our vision in writing the guide is based on the importance of the political participation of women as an essential and crucial entry point into all the levels of authority that will promote protection and safeguard women. We aim at matching and implementing CEDAW 1979 and the Declaration of Beijing of the year 1995 and the methodology stemming from it with Resolution 1325 and all other relevant resolutions.

3.   The importance of Resolution 1325

- The resolution considers that guaranteeing the participation of women in the peace process on all decision making levels and the protection of women is one of the matters most relevant to world peace and security.

- It lays the foundation for the promotion of the equality between men and women in participation and monitoring to draft the constitution, laws, and legislations along with the electoral system, the parties' law,

---

9. Speech by Bashar al Assad at the parliament on June 3rd, 2012. See: https://www.youtube.com/watch?v=WGQczIqsJ3c

and building the police and judiciary sector and all the state institutions and all their levels.

- Resolution 1325 is the first of its kind in that it stipulates the participation of women in the bodies and positions of decision making of a military or security nature. This will lead to a new quality increase in the nature of the role of women and their participation on new unconventional political levels.

- The resolution emphasized that gender based violence, particularly rape and other forms of sexual harm, is a war crime that does not abate with time, and is not included in amnesty laws and relevant legislations; the resolution called for the protection of women in armed conflicts from this type of crime.

- The resolution provided the countries with training materials regarding the protection of women and their rights and private needs; it also encouraged the countries to increase the financial donations to specialized funds and programs.

- Resolution 1325 was enforced as the Security Council adopted four other resolutions, including three that consider sexual violence as a war crime: 1820 year 2008, 1888 year 2009 which was followed by the creation of an office for the personal representative of the General Secretary of the UN for the affairs of sexual violence in conflicts, and as for resolution 1960 of the year 2010, it called for systemic arrangements for monitoring and reporting that enhance the efficiency of tracking the range and severity of these war crimes. The three resolutions (1820, 1888, and 1960) have called for increased efforts by the states that are member of the UN in order to prevent the occurrence of systemic sexual violence, or on a broader scale, during conflicts. Resolution 1889 of the year 2009 is relevant to gender equality and the empowerment of women after the end of conflict in the long term, along with setting indicators to monitor the implementation of Resolution 1325.

4.   Challenges and shortcomings

4.1.   Internationally

- Resolution 1325, similar to many resolutions and agreements of the UN, is not mandatory for member states.

- The politicization of justice and human rights for men and women and the support provided to totalitarian regimes like the Syrian model that committed war crimes and crimes against humanity. Despite all the international and local legal reports that mention those crimes, UN resolutions are drafted with a language that attempts to please all the international players (Resolution 2254) except Syrian men and women. They also omit the fate of the dictator and his aides, nor is there any mention of the transitional justice that cannot be skipped if we are to build a fair and sustainable peace in Syria.

- Resolution 1325 deals with ongoing wars and conflicts as if they were a fatality or a natural disaster we cannot do anything about, even as the UN, despite many warnings that conflicts are often inevitable in many countries of the world that are ruled by totalitarian security regimes like the Syrian model. The crimes and violations have reached alarming levels since the conflict started and have had a great impact on all the countries of the region, including the European Union, as shown by the unprecedented waves of refugees. We cannot stop that wave except via a political solution that puts an end to the tyranny and builds a just, sustainable peace based on holding the war criminals accountable as a starting point to building a democratic state committed to the charter of human rights for men and women. In the Syrian context, we see various attempts to stereotype the role of feminists/women as, on the one side, victims, and on the other they are required to push the males to the negotiations table for a reconciliation of some sort that they call 'peace', in a cloning of the role of women whose country has been through an armed conflict between two teams that want to seize the power and resources: good women that want peace are facing mean men starting wars. This view includes discrimination against men and oversimplifies the role of women as free politicians and rebels that took part in the revolution and face tyranny and the distortion of the required democratic alternative in future Syria. It also understates the major sacrifices that the Syrian people have presented.

4.2. Locally

- The limited awareness of decision makers amongst the Syrian men and women regarding the resolution, even on a leadership level, and the absence of a political will to set women's causes as a priority.

- The absence of trust on the side of the oppressed Syrian men and women in international bodies as they have been let down and are not being given support as refugees, forced emigrants, who were besieged, detained, or forcibly disappeared. Our requests to separate the humanitarian file from the political one are still unheard. The cause of the men and women detained in the detention centers of the regime is our bleeding wound. The exploding barrels are still there along with the prohibited weapons targeting civilians. The regime still practices starving and besieging and forced displacement as a weapon of war. The more the international community talks about a political solution, the more the battles, air raids, bombing of innocents continues, and the more the military bases of the countries involved in the conflict (i.e. Russia, the US, and recently the Turkish army) join. The more they talk in international resolutions about a political solution produced and owned by the Syrians – men and women –, the more they draft resolutions without the participation of Syrian men and women and the more Syrian bloodshed is undermined.

- Religion has always been used to oppress ideas and for political gain, 'cultural specificity' is a term that was always used to oppress half of the society, subdue it, abuse it, and terrorize it. In Syria, the two tyrannies

– political and religious – join forces, mutually support one another, and dominate the public and private sphere. This has lead to the trampling of human rights for men and women, and emptied the society from the politics that was regained by the oppressed revolution that is not being allowed to prevail. All opposition and human rights groups have been banned and chased. All attempts to create a democratic change were aborted and feminist associations were deprived of the possibility to have legal authorizations and from making a noticeable change in the coercive rights ruling their lives. The regime allowed and facilitated the spread and expansion of a religious current that calls for the subjection to rulers and custodians. To understand the Syrian situation, it is enough to review how the constitution was amended in the year 2000 after the death of Hafez al Assad within minutes to fit the age of the heir. On the other hand, a simple change to the personal status laws regarding increasing the age of custody took decades.

References

Al Chaher, C. I. (2015). The political participation of women in Syria. *Naqd wa Tanwir magazine*. https://goo.gl/GwZUcn

Kannout, L. (2017). *In the core or on the margin: Syrian women's political participation*. Syrian Feminist Lobby.

UNHCR. (2014). *Women alone: the fight for survival by Syria's refugee women*. http://www.unhcr.org/ar/53bb8d006.pdf

UNHCR. (2016). *Confronting Fragmentation: Impact of Syrian crisis report*. The Syrian Center for Policy Research. http://scpr-syria.org/publications/policy-reports/confronting-fragmentation/

3 Women's human rights when experiencing humanitarian crises and conflicts: the impact of United Nations Security Council Resolutions on women, peace, security, and the CEDAW General Recommendation no. 30

Paola Degani[1]

Violence and insecurity are strictly linked to unequal political, social, and economic power. However, the continuity of violence is obscured by masculinist and patriarchal rules of security within gendered structures, especially inside the division of public/private dimensions and spaces, of production-reproduction activities, and of conflicts of war/peace.

Nowadays, there is a general perception of the gendered dimensions of humanitarian emergencies in public policy outcomes and more in general in institutional contexts where the central role of women in security and maintaining peace, at all levels of decision making, both prior to, during, and after the conflict stage, hostilities, and peace-keeping and peace-building stages, as well as in trying to pursue a condition of reconciliation and reconstruction, has been formally recognized at international level.

Nevertheless, it is necessary to focus on some problems related to the conceptualization of and legal provision for 'gender based security' and its subsequent effects upon accountability, with particular reference to transitional justice and post-conflict societies. It is important to assess a range of contemporary issues implicated for women and security, such as violence and other forms of harassment in times of post-conflict.

1. University of Padova, Padova, Italy; paola.degani@unipd.it

How to cite this chapter: Degani, P. (2018). Women's human rights when experiencing humanitarian crises and conflicts: the impact of United Nations Security Council Resolutions on women, peace, security, and the CEDAW General Recommendation no. 30. In C. Padovani & F. Helm (Eds), *Rethinking the transition process in Syria: constitution, participation and gender equality* (pp. 39-60). Research-publishing.net. https://doi.org/10.14705/rpnet.2018.21.757

1. On the concept of women's security: introductory notes

For quite a long time now, the scientific literature has addressed the security paradigm(s) and issues without paying adequate attention to the ways in which specific kinds of threats or vulnerabilities may affect certain individuals.

Themes touching on women's insecurity have appeared in institutional and political agendas only in recent years, making visible how the lack of integration of political-military security from socio-economic perspectives determines important consequences for women's rights. Issues classified today under the heading 'gender (women) security' in the political debate at international level have crucial political relevance for the development of public policies aimed at the recognition, respect and effectiveness of human rights in terms of promotion and protection. In this debate, 'security' or 'security sectors' as analytical categories – or political perspectives – are often used as holistic concepts, encompassing both the notion of physical security for women in transitional societies, and a broader notion of human security, based on a relationship between material security, legal security, and political capacity. Indeed, these categories substantially improve and innovate the decision-making and law making processes in the area of security.

The very concept of human security was advanced by the United Nations Development Program (UNDP) in 1994 in the fifth Human Development Report (UNDP, 1994), which included a systematic discussion on security. In that report, the UNPD did not dedicate any specific attention to women, but defined a series of security areas that allow reference to be made to this holistic perspective in order to emphasize and frame an inclusive idea of gender security.

The concept of human security is deliberately protective and proactive. This orientation follows the pathway traced by the United Nations Charter, and by the development of the human rights law at the international level. It does this through a machinery provided for monitoring the effectiveness and the level of implementation, within each single state, of many treaties and other instruments devoted to improving different aspects of human dignity and well-being (Newman & Richmond, 2002).

As mentioned in Degani (2013, p. 5) and in Pividori and Degani (2018), initially, 'human security' presented four main features: the universality of threats, both in type and territorial extension (unemployment, poverty, drugs, crime, terrorism, environmental pollution, human rights violations); an interdependence of its different elements; prevention as a crucial tool in achieving the goals; and centrality of the individual and social groups in satisfying the fundamental needs/rights. In other words, if the human security framework or approach is based first of all on protecting people and communities, in terms of both freedom from fear and freedom from want, this should mean safety from chronic or sudden threats, including sexual violence, hunger, human rights abuses, disease, and repression.

Security, based on a concrete active citizenship, also represents a concrete basis for building a sustainable, peaceful scenario. Following the reasoning put forward by Martha Nussbaum (1997), it is a duty to take a look at the different capabilities of which people are deprived, such as being able to live a long life in good and positive conditions and environments; to engage in all forms of social interaction; to participate, disapprove of, and influence decisions; and to live acquiring a decent standard of living, defined by level of individual security as something holistic and essential for living in dignity.

The complexity of a gender/women perspective in policy areas involving the concept of human security stems from the specific nature of certain risks affecting specifically the woman's condition. The traditional model of security, still understood under the prism of political realism and, its most relevant modification, neorealism, completely neglect women's needs.

So while the primary purpose of addressing gender security remains redressing the imbalance and distortion produced by dominant security discourses and the policies that accompany them, its broader effects may transform the post-conflict environment in unexpected ways. Taking into consideration the preexisting conditions for women, that is women's ordinary experiences in their daily lives, is fundamental when dealing with women's potential vulnerability and specificities in situations of crisis or humanitarian emergencies. Only by acknowledging the ordinary dimension of women's discrimination and subordination is it possible to explain the intersection of women's life experiences and the humanitarian emergencies normally characterized by physical displacement, physical injury requiring medical intervention, inadequate access to food and water, severe psychosocial Post Traumatic Stress Disorder (PTSD) symptoms, and increased evidence of post-event violence directed at vulnerable individuals. Women face particular social and economic problems in conflicts and emergencies that can cause or increase their vulnerability. For many, the relationship between the abusive and violent practice and situations experienced during conflict and the security of the post-conflict environment are not discontinuous realities, but rather part of a single experience defined by discrimination and abuse rooted in the cultural and social context of many of the countries involved in situations of emergencies and transition.

Gender dichotomy (the division and the difference between male and female in terms of social roles and attitudes) is first of all characterized by hierarchies that are rooted, to various degrees, in the various social and cultural contexts. This phenomenon implicates important repercussions increasing inequality and polarization, and deepening the hierarchies that have historically characterized the sexual and international division of labor. The issue of women's equality reflects this complexity, since the discriminations and some widespread and very common forms of violations of human rights still affecting women make them more vulnerable to individual and social conditions that are incompatible with an holistic, authentic, and coherent perspective of 'human security' (Degani, 2013; Pividori & Degani, 2018).

The 1990's represents a very important historical moment both in the process of multiplication and progressive elaboration of rights, and in promoting and protecting human rights, particularly women's rights. But in parallel there have been drastic changes in the social and economic status of women generating enormous discrepancies based on gender. Different kind of emergencies, however, have recently created the conditions for developing greater awareness concerning the insecurity of women. Such crises also include the recent and ongoing economic and financial recession, even in European countries, where the migration processes today increase the contradictions that many states face in this political moment: changes involving labor relations; female migration with new patterns and trends, in its different expressions; the trafficking of young women for forced prostitution and the proliferation of sex businesses on an industrial scale; the extent of conflicts based on ethnic discriminations; ideological and religious fundamentalisms and intolerance; and the diffusion of violence as a social reality transversally added to all the other peculiarities that might characterize women. Such situations of crisis over the last 20 years have brought about a radical change in how women's security is framed and evaluated. The need to prohibit and punish a series of conducts, now recognized by international criminal law as crimes against humanity or war crimes (and/ or genocide) in times of war, has been formally acknowledged. The feminist concept of violence as well as its causes, in times of peace, have been re-framed as problems where the public and the private dimensions intermesh and influence one another, both on the level of values and on a material level, also involving the *Due Diligence* standard (Pividori & Degani, 2018).

2. Gender security issues within the human security paradigm

On a strictly politico-institutional level, it is possible to define distinct stages in the evolving notion of human security and the progressive affirmation of a paradigm authentically different from the traditional realist view. This phase coincided with the Agenda for Peace presented in 1992 by the Secretary General of the United Nations (UN), Boutros Boutros-Ghali, followed in 1995 by the Supplement to the Agenda for Peace that re-proposed the goals already mentioned in 1992. During those same years, while the search for new political instruments for peace and international security continued, new interest in other dimensions of human insecurity that gave evidence to women's realities grew.

Women have responsibilities related to human care in most societies and also disproportionately bear familial and communal care responsibilities in communities affected by disaster, war, and humanitarian and natural emergencies. Among the different states and across jurisdictions, women possess different levels of legal capacity to engage in legal contracts, face systematic discrimination in their access to employment, receive differential payment once employed, and meet obstructions as regards their own or transferral of property.

These different, multiple, interlocking and intersectional discriminations, and the need to combat them, are recognized in the International Convention on the Elimination of All Forms of Discrimination Against Women (CEDAW) through the observations and jurisprudence produced by the committee foreseen by the convention to monitor its implementation among state parties.

Beyond a doubt, the international political arena's activities in promoting the status of women proceed in a globalized context marked by the advancement of neo-liberal policies, which seem to aggravate gender inequalities rather than favor an improvement in women's standards of living.

In particular, the reproduction of human beings, which is the foundation of every economic and political system, and the enormous amount of paid and unpaid domestic work done daily by women in the home (and in the informal economy), is what permits the world to evolve and to perform and respond to different challenges. From a feminist perspective, this issue postpones and calls for the transformation of our everyday life and the creation of new forms of solidarity (Dalla Costa, 1973; Federici, 2012).

Numerous opinions today denounce an overall worsening of the woman's condition due to policies of deregulation and privatization and the direct effects and the mechanisms they have triggered, dismantling social welfare structures and reducing the quality level of social reproduction and incomes.

With regard to gender security, an increasing political awareness of male violence against women sheds light on the urgent need to intervene at various levels. Degani (2013) further states that "[w]ith reference to the conflicts of the 1990's, to traditional practices affecting women and to the consequences of poverty, unemployment and precarious living conditions, the need to discuss the issue of violence against women in terms of security crisis appears evident" (p. 10). Male violence against women is a universal problem, despite the peculiarities marking the various geographic and social contexts as a consequence of gender inequalities.

Violence against women can be viewed as a turning point between male and female insecurity that allowed us to seize one of the main critical issues for human rights today.

The linkage between patriarchal structures and culture with violence is much more complex than would appear at first sight due to the fact that violence takes shape within a continuum of power that sometimes makes it difficult to distinguish among different forms, fluctuations, and phases. "Inequality is tied to violence with a double cord. First of all, inequality breeds and favors violence, which is an expression or effect of inequality itself. Second, inequality is fuelled and fostered by violence" (Degani, 2013, p. 12). Violence also represents the real gap between a 'male' and 'female' concept of human security, and is the most significant manifestation of systemic conditions of discrimination.

In humanitarian crises, the widespread risk of violence against women can be framed from a perspective of unequal gender relationships in both the family and society. There can be an escalation of specific forms of violence against women in societies experiencing armed conflict (Fisher, 2010).

Violence against women can be observed as a means of warfare in such contexts, precisely intended to target the civilian community. In humanitarian emergencies, since the early stage, women become even more vulnerable to violence as a result of fraying social structures and the collapse of political and legal systems, but more specifically because they normally lack protective instruments and social structure (Ní Aoláin, 2009, 2011).

The international community's efforts to contrast male violence against women based on gender, formally announced during the World Human Rights Conference in Vienna in 1993, are summarized in the Declaration on the Elimination of Violence against Women, adopted by the General Assembly in the same year and in the appointment by the former United Nations Human Rights Commission (UNHRC) of the Special Rapporteur on violence against women. The work of this last mechanism was remarkable during the 1990's and in the following years, and today represents a very important input in updating political agendas on this matter (Charlesworth, 1990; Degani, 2000; Sullivan, 1994).

The relevance attributed to the issue of violence against women and more in general towards populations struck by humanitarian emergencies is partly linked to the strong media impact of a number of emergencies during the 1990's (Pickup, Williams, & Sweetman, 2001). Reference here is made in particular to ethnic conflicts where sexual violence was used as an instrument of war.

In this historical phase, the conflict in Syria, and the resulting refugee crisis in the Middle East, has placed many girls and women at risk of different forms of violence, exploitation, and insecurity. More than 75% of the Syrian refugees who have fled to neighboring countries are women and children (UNHCR, 2016b).

According to the UN, Gender-Based Violence (GBV), including child marriage, is the main issue currently experienced by girls and women in Syria and hosting countries, and trafficking linked to smuggling of migrants in the context of mixed migrations is on the increase. Without a doubt, the dimension assumed today by this phenomenon indicates the absolute necessity of reinforcing international instruments devoted to the protection of women's rights in order to avoid conflict related to situations that affect women who have been forcibly displaced, especially those on the move to seek asylum. This implies framing better the acts committed against women and girls as part of genocidal violence, war crimes, and crimes against humanity.

From a historical point of view, the condition of women in armed conflicts has not been the object of specific attention under international law. Sexual violence in armed conflict is, of course, forbidden and sanctioned under international humanitarian law but the efficacy of these provisions in preventing and identifying accountability for these crimes remains unconvincing, although the new great attention towards victims of severe crimes in international human rights and in the criminal law drawn up by the European Union and the Council of Europe is promising.

3. Women, peace, and security: beyond the symbolic dimension

From the very start, United Nations activities for the promotion of the status of women and the protection of women's rights have been characterized by the link between peace, development, and equality. Reconsideration of three fundamental policy elements in a holistic manner was needed starting from the First World Conference on the International Women's Year held in Mexico City in 1975, even though a more elaborated conceptualization of the issue at the policy level was only developed in the framework of the Third World Conference on Women in Nairobi in 1985. As stated in Degani (2013), in subsequent years, "the elaboration of the linkages between these three objectives (peace, development, equality) formed the basis for the political discussion and activity not only of the women's movement but also of international institutions devoted to the protection of human rights" (p. 19) and more specifically those which was/is related to the promotion of women, such as the UN Commission on the Status of Women.

Institutional feminists, in particular advocacy activities for peace, have called for the equal participation of women and men in decision making associated with conflict resolution and peacemaking, underlining the importance of gender equality as a value in itself and in opposition to the lack of physical security and the persistence of discriminatory social norms that reproduce and legitimate violence against women both in private and public dimensions.

In practical terms, the prevalence of violence that women in transitional societies experience, both in the public and private spheres, can be contrasted not only by placing barriers to state or public violence directed against them. There is, rather, a fundamental need to promote transformative actions against violence and its underlying causes in the private sphere, as part of a more holistic transformative and inclusive project. This situation needs to change, not only because it is a source of major global injustice in the world, but also because poverty is sexist, and poverty (of resources and rights) is the primary cause of women's vulnerability in emergencies. Poverty and gender inequality are on the same line.

> "Of fundamental importance is the recognition of the role of women in situations of crisis and of their struggle to contribute to the well-being of their communities. [...] An equitable gender representation in peace negotiations should ensure the social legitimization of such decision-making processes and [...] provide for more acceptable solutions to those members of society bearing the highest costs of war, [thus offering women a chance for advancement in numerous areas related to their rights]" (Degani, 2013, p. 20).

4. Women's security in the framework of UN Security Council resolutions

Through the adoption of the United Nations Security Council Resolution (UNSCR)1325 and the subsequent UNSCRs, the Women, Peace, and Security (WPS) agenda identifies three priority issues: the representation of women at all levels of peace and security governance; the significant participation of women in peace and security governance; and the protection of women's rights and bodies in conflict and post-conflict situations (Shepherd, 2014).

In relation to these issues, the UNSCR 1325 on Women and Peace and Security, adopted in 2000, signs an important stage towards the recognition of the supporting role and capacity of women in the prevention and resolution of conflicts and in encouraging the expansion of their contribution to international policing missions. The resolution thus recognizes women's conceivable contribution to peace, in conflict resolution and, more generally, in assisting post-war reconstruction efforts and the rehabilitation of victims. UNSCR 1325 recognizes that men and women experience security differently and that to build sustainable peace, women need to be fully involved.

In its 18 paragraphs, the resolution expresses the commitment of the most important body responsible for the maintenance of peace and security in the international community to enhance the involvement and full participation of women in all efforts towards peace and security.

In this important document, which recognizes the different experiences of women and men with regard to security and peace, the Security Council prompts the States to focus more on gender-sensitive issues when training the peacekeeping personnel, and urges all parties to armed conflict to fully respect international law applicable to the rights and protection of women and girls. Clearly this implies that there be a Security Sector Reform (SSR) that meets the different security needs recognizing different gender attitudes in terms of men, women, boys, girls, and others too.

> "Resolution 1325, given its wide-ranging goals and unanimous approval, is considered a milestone in that it inaugurated a new kind of commitment which from 2000 has led to the adoption of other important resolutions in the area. [...] It is thus evident that the growing attention towards populations struck by humanitarian emergencies must adequately address the gender dimension in peace negotiations if such interventions are to be effective" (Degani, 2013, p. 22).

Over the last two decades, the UNSC has adopted other resolutions that highlight some of the particular consequences of armed conflict afflicting women and girls, and which emphasize the idea of an active role in transition processes, in disarmament, demobilization, reintegration, and, more in general, in reforming the security sector. In real terms, these documents do not challenge effectively the 'patriarchy' and masculine culture structures of the transitional justice reforms/ processes, nor do they pay sufficient attention to the link between ordinary and extra-ordinary violence against women. First of all, according to Puechguirbal

(2010), the re-proposition of stereotyping language in these texts sometimes risks removing women's agency keeping them in the subordinated position of victims. As a result, women are not seen as actors within their own community and agents of change in post-conflict environments. As discussed in Martín de la Rosa and Domínguez Romero (2014),

> "[t]he representation of women in these resolutions plays down female agency, articulating a feminine subject that in times of conflict is the target of sexual violence, [and other severe forms of sexual abuses in particular in the context of forced prostitution and human trafficking.] In times of peace they just reproduce the roles assigned to them in the power hierarchy, where they are subordinated and dependent [on a male (with different status)]. In other words, as stated by Shepherd (2011), it can be said that the discursive representation of gender assumed in these documents reproduces roles where women [appear] fragile, passive, and in need of protection, and men as [breadwinners who have always had the decision-making power and the responsibility of providing] needed protection to women, [as foreseen by the social, cultural rules and in some situations by law systems too]" (p. 59).

This situation contributes to a complete lack of awareness about the real nature of the ordinary private violence experienced by women and arising from usual dimensions of subordination and discrimination, which is totally dissociated from the wider issues of control being exercised in society. Differently, focusing upon women's potential to fill active roles in the political transformation, women's participation should be vital both in contributing to solve the crisis and in making sure that women's interests and needs are addressed in every agreement and political choice moving forward. In many places around the world as commonly recognized, war can be a turning point for female empowerment. As men are absent, fighting or killed, women move out of their traditional roles.

In November 2011, a UNFPA report found that one in three women in Syria experienced domestic violence and several Syrian laws clearly disadvantage women; the penalty for 'honor' killing is softer than for other murders, and there is no legislation that specifically prohibits gender discrimination (UNFPA, 2011). The Syrian family code limits women's financial rights within marriage if they work outside the home without their husbands' consent. In other words, Syrian women have to fight against patriarchy, dictatorship, and also religious extremism. In these circumstances, it is explicit that women's participation could also be needed to improve reporting on gender-specific impacts of violence to struggle against the reproduction of the structural dimensions and causes that continue to improve severe forms of women's human rights violations.

All the acts provide guidance for states, regional organizations, the UN system and other stakeholders in addressing the needs of women and girls during and after armed conflict, and in promoting their empowerment, stressing the importance of protecting women by preventing conflict-related sexual violence and other abuses.

The UNSC resolutions adopted after Resolution 1325 in general are focused on the peculiar negative effects of armed conflict on women, the potential of women's contribution to peace, security, and reconciliation, and the need to combat male violence against women declining these specific aspects with more or less importance and deepened differently.

A few days after the adoption of UNSCR 1325, in adopting another resolution, Resolution 1327 (2000), the UNSC re-emphasized the importance of the Secretary-General in conflict prevention and reaffirmed the role of women in conflict prevention, resolution, and peace-building.

The adoption of this act was followed by others, first UNSCR 1820, adopted in June 2008, which underlines the need for special measures to protect women and girls from sexual violence in armed conflict, and to ensure access to justice and assistance for victims while also emphasizing the role of peacekeepers in protecting civilians and advocating an increase in the number of female peacekeepers.

UNSCR 1888, adopted in September 2009, focuses on the inclusion of sexual violence issues in peace processes, and on addressing impunity in order to ensure access to justice for survivors. It also defines new mechanisms within the UN to intensify the struggle against war-related sexual violence, and foresees the establishment of a Special Representative of the Secretary-General on the issue.

After this document, UNSCR 1889, adopted in October 2009, widens the Council's focus on and commitment to women's participation in peace-building, emphasizing the role of women in political and economic decision-making. Differently, Resolution 1960, adopted in 2010, establishes a monitoring, analysis, and reporting mechanism on conflict-related sexual violence, and calls upon parties to armed conflict to make specific, time-bound commitments to prohibit and punish this crime, also asking the Secretary-General to monitor those commitments. Meanwhile, UNSCR 2106, adopted in 2013, reiterates its demand for the complete suspension, with immediate effect by all parties to armed conflict, of all acts of sexual violence and it calls for these parties to make and implement specific due date commitments to combat sexual violence focusing on accountability for perpetrators (Pividori & Degani, 2018).

In the same year, UNSCR 2122 aims at strengthening women's role in all stages of conflict prevention and resolution and in addressing the persistent gaps in the implementation of WPS agendas, expresses the will to increase the attention, making reference in particular to the protection of civilians in armed conflict, to post-conflict peace-building, to strengthening the promotion of the rule of law, and to the threats caused by terrorist acts.

In the last years, the UNSC has adopted two other resolutions on this topic: in October 2015, UNSCR 2242, on women's roles in countering violent extremism and terrorism, and in March 2016, UNSCR 2272, on sexual exploitation and abuse in peace operations.

Recently, the position expressed by the CEDAW Committee on the 18th of October 2013 with the General Recommendation (GR) no. 30 on women in conflict prevention, conflict and post-conflict situations, reaffirms the link between the principle of non-discrimination and the urgent need to recognize the specificity of women's condition in the situation of humanitarian crises and conflicts.

5. Recent developments: on the CEDAW Committee General Recommendation no. 30

As is known, CEDAW has used this form of soft law to support a correct and coherent interpretation within the human rights perspective of the contents of the convention by the member states (Kois, 1999). CEDAW GRs in recent years in particular have made a progressive adaptation of the text of the convention possible with the evolution of the principle of gender/sex-based discrimination. This has been done through a progressive integration of a relevant number of issues and by updating the interpretations with regard to many topics from the entry into force of the convention and with it the CEDAW committee.

This GR improves synergies between WPS and broader human rights duties. With this act, the committee called on CEDAW state parties to guarantee that implementation of their WPS efforts will consider within the broader equality and women's rights obligations of CEDAW. Further, state parties are called to report on implementation of their WPS commitments in their periodic reports to CEDAW. GR no. 30 specifies that

> "the general recommendation covers the application of the Convention to conflict prevention, international and non-international armed conflicts, situations of foreign occupation, as well as other forms of occupation and the post-conflict phase. In addition, the Recommendation covers other situations of concern, such as internal disturbances, protracted and low intensity civil strife, political strife, ethnic and communal violence, states of emergency and suppression of mass uprisings, war against terrorism and organized crime, that may not necessarily be classified as armed conflict under international humanitarian law and which result in serious violations of women's rights and are of particular concern to the Committee" (CEDAW, 2013, p. 2).

The structure of this document is highly technical. It offers an extensive interpretation of the convention's content and develops a coherent approach that confirms the continuum of work carried out by the committee in recent years directed towards the structuring of increasing affirmation of the due diligence standard. The specificity of this document is with no doubt represented by the political need and opportunity of the CEDAW committee to identify the impact of the convention declining more deeply in terms of "women's human rights", a list of issues normally and implicitly included within WPS agendas today. With the aim of polishing every ambiguity about these matters, the committee offers a holistic perspective and a genuine interpretation to states operating on these situations and contexts.

Particularly, the general standard of the *due diligence* and the perspective of a duty to protect women based on this political framework should help intergovernmental organizations reinforce the commitment towards more concrete efforts in protecting women and supporting their fundamental capacities.

GR no. 30 is a document that definitely frames issues related to the status of women in different humanitarian emergency situations in a more complex manner compared with the different acts adopted by the UNSC. Through a progressive integration of a number of acts and situations within the concept of discrimination, and with the consequential duties under the convention, the committee progressively increases the political relevance and the holistic character of the convention content offering women a more adequate protection of their rights. And there is no doubt of the very high symbolic dimensions in these documents of CEDAW's commitment in this phase, but it is absolutely undeniable that this treaty body has in recent years acquired a much stronger legitimacy than in the past.

To sum up, the GR considers the possibility offered by the convention in conflict prevention, conflict and post-conflict situations, the application to state and non-state actors, the complementarity with the international humanitarian, refugee and criminal laws, and with the UNSC agenda on women, peace, and security, and the monitoring and reporting system in relation to the treaty ratification.

Many issues are taken into consideration in the text: conflict prevention, male violence, human-trafficking, participatory attitudes, level of education, employment opportunities, and health services. For rural women too: displacement, refugees and asylum-seekers, security sector reforms, disarmament, demobilization and reintegration, constitutional and electoral reform, access to justice, nationality and statelessness, and marriage and family relations.

6.   To conclude: on the state of the art

The approach proposed by the international community on the issue of human security and the status of women, categorically overcomes the traditional perspective of the relationship between the gender issues and armed conflicts, emphasizing, on the other hand, the impact of armed conflicts on the civil population and in particular on women and girls with a particular emphasis on the role of sexual violence. Contrary to the view that wars and humanitarian emergencies are distinguished phenomena that do not interfere with women's lives and the human reproductive dimension, it is acknowledged that they deeply impact the female population.

Considering that women have a greater risk of dying and being injured than fighters seems to point to the significant way in which armed conflicts have changed over time.

Disarmament, demobilization, and social reintegration during the transition phase are today included in the political agenda of the international community, as is the problem of forced displacement. This is underscored by the High Commissioner for Refugees data (UNHCR, 2016a) that illustrates the fact that women and girls are among those seeking in great proportion humanitarian protection. This also implies that trafficking in human beings, due to the features of the migration processes today, finds a favorable ground in situations of conflicts. On their journeys, the migrants who flee from their country of origin towards European nations using the Balkan route, especially in countries like Greece and former Yugoslav Republic of

Macedonia, have a high probability of encountering situations of violence, extortion, and exploitation, including rape, transactional sex, and human and organ trafficking. Women and girls, especially those travelling alone, face particularly high risks of certain forms of violence, including sexual violence by smugglers, criminal groups, and individuals in countries along the route. As of November 2015, per government figures, 950,469 refugees and migrants had arrived in Europe through the Mediterranean, with the vast majority of these arriving to Greece (797,372). According with UNHCR (2016a) statistical data, approximately, 24 percent are children and 16 percent are women, while 3,605 have either lost their lives or are missing. Although the existing research and progress made in the work against sexual gender based violence, there is still a perception among many humanitarian actors that these facts are not a feature of this crisis due to a lack of data on its incidents and due to the tentative of the victims to avoid disclosing this experience and seeking assistance unless there is a severe and visible health implication. As described in the report produced by the Special Rapporteur of the Human Rights Council on trafficking in persons (UNHRC, 2016, p. 8), since 2011, an increased number of Syrian refugees have been trafficked for purposes of labor exploitation in the agricultural, industry, manufacturing, catering, and informal sectors in Jordan, Lebanon, and Turkey. Women and girls seeking to survive in conflict zones are often compelled to exchange sexual services and even to "marry" for food, shelter, protection, or safe passage. UNHCR (2016a, p. 11) has recognized and denounced that women in conflict situations are vulnerable to a range of discriminatory practices that increase their dependence (for example, receiving smaller food rations or not having ration cards or other identity documents in their own name) and are disproportionately exposed to sexual violence. The trafficking of women and girls for sexual exploitation, which frequently implies such acts as sexual slavery, forced marriage, forced prostitution, and forced pregnancy, features within the broader scenario of sexual violence perpetrated against the civilian population during and in the wake of conflicts. Perhaps the link between trafficking in women and girls and sexual violence is clearly recognized today at institutional levels and in many international instruments. As the same Special Rapporteur has underlined presenting her report during the

General Assembly 71st session (UNHRC, 2016, p.12), although some form of abduction has been a feature of armed conflicts in the past, recently there has been an extreme arrangement of abducting women and girls from their homes or schools in conflict-affected contexts and areas. These women and girls may subsequently be forced to marry and/or work as sex slaves. Such exploitation, in some cases, also involves trafficking for forced and recently for shamed marriage and sexual enslavement by religious and political extremist groups.

In order to prevent such kidnappings, families are reported to be confining women and girls and removing girls from school. Trafficking for the purpose of forced prostitution does not represent an act perpetrated only by organized criminal groups. For instance, the Special Rapporteur's (UNHRC, 2016, p. 12) report underlines that Syrian refugee women and girls may be trafficked for sexual exploitation through the practice of "temporary" or child and/or forced marriages. They may be obliged by their parents to marry and these arrangements are a way of securing their daughters' safety and *safeguarding* the family's maintenance through the bride price. Once married, such wives are likely to end up in a situation of sexual and domestic exploitation. Trafficking for forced prostitution through marriages with foreign men who then force their "brides" into prostitution in another country is common.

Sexual violence contributes to exacerbate the difficulties of the families to adapt their life during armed conflicts. It should be considered that:

> "one of the consequences of humanitarian emergencies and current migration flows is the phenomenon of family disintegration. In this context, a large number of family households, often including elderly or persons with disabilities, are headed by and thus totally dependent [on a woman]. Once again, then, strengthening [women's] economic security status [and personal capacity], thus promoting their economic, social, and cultural rights, is of fundamental importance. It would not only enable women to fully participate in decision-making processes, whether in times of emergency or transition, but it also confers full citizenship upon them" (Degani, 2013, p. 25).

Instead of advancing a paradigm of security centered on military control, security should be framed as a part of the wider move towards global governance, becoming an all-encompassing condition in which individuals live in safety and in dignity.

What is certain is that the number of relevant situations on the humanitarian level in the world, the spread of conflicts and complex emergency crises suggest that giving effect to the content of these acts seems difficult. It is necessary to build an idea of real sustainability of international political processes that focuses on the person; one which re-proposes a new social welfare policy through the research of a new world order project, capable of solving the humanitarian crises that we are living today, and it is necessary to consider that gendered inequalities and discriminations between men and women should be part of the same global frameworks for bringing about lasting peace and a real people-centered approach towards security.

For women, safety requires a comprehensive reflection on the system of inequalities and a general political effort towards more equitable societies in terms of human rights and access to resources.

Regarding the main causes of male violence, they involve redefining the social structures and community systems. Moreover, women's autonomy, their decision-making skills, and their empowerment also need to be reinforced. A proper understanding of violence against women within the patriarchal structures of society allows for a politicization of issues related to violence, and for a concrete elimination of the obstacles that do not permit women to live in dignity.

References

CEDAW. (2013). *General recommendation No. 30 on women in conflict prevention, conflict and post-conflict situations.* CEDAW/C/GC/30. UN Committee on the Elimination of Discrimination Against Women. http://www.refworld.org/docid/5268d2064.html

Charlesworth, H. (1990). The UN declaration on violence against women. *Social Justice, 17*, 53-70.

Dalla Costa M. (1973). Women and the subversion of the community. In M. Dalla Costa & S. James (Eds), *The power of women and the subversion of the community.* Falling Wall Press.

Degani, P. (2000). *Diritti umani e violenza contro le donne: recenti sviluppi in materia di tutela internazionale*, Quaderno n. 1, Centro di studi e di formazione sui diritti della persona e dei popoli. Università di Padova. http://unipd-centrodirittiumani.it/public/docs/quaderno_02.pdf

Degani, P. (2013). Gender security between human development and human security. Recent Issues in the Political International Agenda. In I. Testoni et al. (Eds), *Against gender based violence from italian debate to intercultural dialogue.* Filema Ed.

Federici S. (2012). *Revolution at point zero: housework, reproduction, and feminist struggle.* PM Press/Common Notions/Autonomedia.

Fisher, S. (2010). Violence against women and natural disasters: findings from post-tsunami Sri Lanka. *Violence Against Women, 16*(8), 902-918. https://doi.org/10.1177/1077801210377649

Kois, L. M. (1999). Violence against women. In K. D. Askin & D. Koenig (Eds), *Women and international human rights law.* Transnational Publishers.

Martín de la Rosa, V., & Domínguez Romero, E. (2014). Is the portrayal of women's role changing in United Nations peacekeeping resolutions? *International Journal of Humanities and Social Science, 4*(11), 54-63. http://ijhssnet.com/journals/Vol_4_No_11_1_September_2014/7.pdf?

Ní Aoláin, F. (2009). Women, security, and the patriarchy of internationalized transitional justice. *Human Rights Quarterly, 31*, 1055-1085. https://doi.org/10.1353/hrq.0.0114

Ní Aoláin, F. (2011). Women vulnerability, and humanitarian emergencies. *Michigan Journal of Gender and Law, 18*(1), 1-23. http://repository.law.umich.edu/mjgl/vol18/iss1/1

Newman, E., & Richmond, O. (2002). *The United Nations and human security.* Palgrave McMillan.

Nussbaum, M. C. (1997). Capabilities and human rights. *Fordham Law Review*, 66(2), 273-300. http://ir.lawnet.fordham.edu/flr/vol66/iss2/2

Pickup, F., Williams, S., & Sweetman, C. (2001). *Ending violence against women: a challenge for development and humanitarian work.* Oxfam GB.

Pividori, C., & Degani, P. (2018, FirstView). Reflecting on criminalizing male violence against women under human rights and human security discourses: a feminist legal and policy analysis. *Global Jurist*, 1-12. https://doi.org/10.1515/gj-2017-0028

Puechguirbal, N. (2010). Discourses on gender, patriarchy and Resolution 1325: a textual analysis of UN documents. *International Peacekeeping, 17*(2), 172-187 . https://doi.org/10.1080/13533311003625068

Shepherd, L. J. (2011). Sex, security and superhero(ines): from 1325 to 1820 and beyond. *International Feminist, Journal of Politics*, 13(4), 504-521. https://doi.org/10.1080/146 16742.2011.611659

Shepherd, L. J. (2014). Advancing the women, peace and security agenda: 2015 and beyond. Norwegian Peacebuilding Resource Centre Expert Analysis, August 28. https://noref.no/Publications/Themes/Gender-and-inclusivity/Advancing-the-Women-Peace-and-Security-agenda-2015-and-beyond

Sullivan, D. J. (1994). Women's rights and the 1993 world conference on human rights. *American Journal of International Law*, 88, 152-167. https://doi.org/10.2307/2204032

UNDP (1994). New dimensions of human security. In UNDP (Eds), *Human Development Report 1994*. Oxford University Press. https://doi.org/10.18356/213f0e70-en

UNFPA (2011). The State of World Population 2011. People and possibilities in a world of 7 billion, United Nations Population Fund, 2011. https://doi.org/10.18356/cbd2a655-en

UNHCR. (2016a). U*nited Nations population fund, women's refugee commission. Initial assessment report: protection risks for women and girls in the European refugee and migrant crisis.* Greece and the former Yugoslav Republic of Macedonia. United Nations Refugee Agency. http://www.unhcr.org/569f8f419.pdf

UNHCR. (2016b, January 20). *Refugee women on the move in Europe are at risk.* United Nations Refugee Agency. http://www.unhcr.org/news/latest/2016/1/569fb22b6/refugee-women-move-europe-risk-says-un.html

UNHRC. (2016). *Trafficking in persons, especially women and children.* Report of the Special Rapporteur of the Human Rights Council A/71/303. https://reliefweb.int/sites/reliefweb.int/files/resources/N1625078.pdf

4 Transitional justice, constitution making, and gender equality in a post conflict Syria

Sara Pennicino[1]

We are all well aware of the fact that the war in Syria is still far from an end and therefore one might think that addressing the issue of post conflict transitional justice with specific reference to gender equality might appear very abstract and disconnected from reality. This criticism is certainly not unfounded, however, it cannot be ignored that one of the recommendations of the Independent International Commission of Inquiry on the Syrian Arab Republic, established on the 22nd of August 2011 by the Human Rights Council[2], is to "[t]ake appropriate action by referring the situation to justice, possibly to the International Criminal Court or an *ad hoc* tribunal" (emphasis added, UNHRC, 2017, para. 147).

As a constitutional lawyer, I would therefore like to contribute to the debate herein by framing the mutual influence of transitional justice and constitutionalism, understood as the set of fundamental, constitutive legal standards and practices, with specific attention to the enhancement of gender equality in constitution making. Bridging political transitions and constitution drafting is one of the keys to unleashing long term effects of inclusive and transformative peace-building, with regard to systemic gender inequality. Accordingly, I will first address the concept of transitional justice and its developments and then move to analyze its relationship with constitutionalism.

Finally, although I will not specifically focus on the United Nations Security Council Resolution (UNSCR 1325) or the Convention on the Elimination of All Forms of Discrimination against Women (CEDAW) as tools for moving

1. University of Padova, Padova, Italy; sara.pennicino@unipd.it

2. The Independent International Commission of Inquiry on the Syrian Arab Republic was established on the 22nd of August 2011 by the Human Rights Council through resolution S-17/1 adopted at its 17th special session with a mandate to investigate all alleged violations of international human rights laws since March 2011 in the Syrian Arab Republic.

How to cite this chapter: Pennicino, S. (2018). Transitional justice, constitution making and gender equality in a post conflict Syria. In C. Padovani & F. Helm (Eds), *Rethinking the transition process in Syria: constitution, participation and gender equality* (pp. 61-69). Research-publishing.net. https://doi.org/10.14705/rpnet.2018.21.758

the gender equality agenda forward in conflict and post-conflict contexts, it is important to note that both documents identify constitution-making as a necessary step in improving the status of women and girls in these scenarios; CEDAW (1979) Article 2 calls upon states to "embody the principle of the equality of men and women in their national constitutions", while UNSCR 1325 paragraph 8.c urges "the protection of and respect for human rights of women and girls, particularly as they relate to the constitution"[3]. I will make my final remarks on why and how this relationship is relevant for the inclusion of gender equality in constitution making.

1.   Transitional justice

In her groundbreaking work, Ruti Teitel (2003) explains transitional justice as "the view of justice associated with periods of political change, as reflected in the phenomenology of primarily legal responses that deal with the wrongdoing of repressive regimes" (p. 893). With antecedents in the post-Second World War trials at Nuremberg and the South African Truth and Reconciliation Commission, transitional justice has developed over the 20th century, showing the urgency for a more comprehensive approach aimed at guaranteeing accountability beyond the State. In other words, "transitional justice is [today] an encompassing term that refers to the normative, legal, and political concerns around how post-authoritarian and post-conflict societies provide accountability for the human rights violations of the past, while also consolidating a transition away from political violence" (O'Rourke, 2013, p. 17).

Developments in transitional justice have also played, and will continue to play, a role in changing the content of constitutionalism. Indeed, 20th century constitutionalism was shaped around a demand for limited government and its essential task was that of defining the ambit of applicability of constitutional norms according to the principle of separation of powers and judicial review. Liberal constitutionalism was modelled on a "pre-commitment and constraint on

---

3. S.C.Res.1325, paragraph 8, U.N.Doc.S/RES/1325 (Oct. 31, 2000).

governmental and state action, usually in the name of individual rights" (Teitel, 2014, p. 57), while, on the contrary, contemporary constitutionalism shows a growing concern with accountability for action (and inaction) of the state and also of non-state actors. In fact, "accountability appears not to be exhausted or fulfilled either by rights against the state or by democratic self-determination" (Teitel, 2014, p. 58), as is evident from core approaches to normative and judicial protection of rights in 21st century constitutional systems. A great contribution to this change can be ascribed to the evolution of the concept of state responsibility in international law; indeed, the latter has progressively expanded the meaning of state action as a primal concern of constitutional law.

For well-known historical reasons, 20th century constitutionalism had its focus on abusive conduct of the state, while more recent trends show evidence of a demand for further understanding of responsibility beyond the state. This evolving conception has also been informed by contemporary developments in transitional justice, especially with regard to overlapping areas between international law and international humanitarian law. As an example, one may think of CEDAW, which reaches out well beyond state action into the private sphere, i.e. where discrimination is at stake, and how this international convention expanded individual responsibility. As a result, constitutional obligations are impacted in terms of the "evolution of substantive norms of accountability in the changing parameters surrounding the protection of non-state actors in interstate affairs" (Teitel, 2014, p. 59).

It should be noted that "the momentum of this reciprocal influence, which ultimately makes a mark at [the] constitutional level, is also the result of the increasingly prominent dimension of the combined internationalization and judicialization of transitional justice" (Teitel, 2014, p. 59). In fact, when politics cannot work out a solution in a post-conflict context, victims' groups and other civil society organizations refer to transnational institutions in order to seek reparation. On the contrary, in the past, these situations, as difficult as they might have been, were resolved largely in domestic *fora*. For example, "both South Africa and Argentina's transitional justice arrangements were the product of multiple stages of political bargaining and, particularly in South Africa, processes of constitution making, including processes of democratic ratification, and consensus over commitments concerning what values should guide the transition"[4].

Having said this, the internationalization of transitional justice is not limited to the role of adjudicatory bodies, but it involves international organizations and Non-Governmental Organizations (NGOs) at a transnational level who interact with local NGOs and other organized groups, especially victims' groups. This combination of levels calls for specific attention to the context in order to deliver true justice, i.e. justice as understood in that specific context. One possible approach is that of Rwanda, with the combined prosecutions by the International *ad hoc* tribunal and the *Gacaca* Court system – justice in the grass – at a local level.

2. Transitional justice and constitution making

The mainly backward looking aims of transitional justice and the forward looking ones of constitution making are linked. However, depending on what approach is adopted towards transitional justice, the constitutional outcome may differ. For example, a strictly restorative approach to transitions has the objective of restoring the *status quo ante* and will therefore orient the type of constituent process in both procedural (who is involved, is it shared with the polity, etc.) and substantive (content wise) terms. On the contrary, there should be a transitional commitment to transformation in order for the constitutional change to represent the legal response to the past regime on the road to liberalization.

But what is the link between this commitment and constitutional change? "A transitional context itself lends the constitutional project an implicit teleology" (Teitel, 2014, p. 61), meaning that the way transitional justice is handled and delivered shapes the constitutional self. South Africa is again the best example,

---

4. See Azanian Peoples Org. and Others v. President of the Republic of S. Afr. 1996 (8) BCLR 1015 (CC) and Azanian Peoples Org. and Others v. Truth and Reconciliation Commission 1996 (4) SA 562 (CC) (upholding amnesty agreement against victim's challenge).

with its case of *ubuntu* – the art of humanity –; the inclusion of social rights in the Constitution, and the recognition of cultural and linguistic rights in both individualistic and communal terms. In countries that did not follow the path of Truth and Reconciliation Commissions (TRC) or other forms of transition justice, history tells us that many years after the end of the transition, questions about victims and perpetrators of past-regimes' abuses are still in the spotlight of attention[5]. However, a best practice approach based on the idea that a TRC model should be universally applicable to grant a successful transition is evidently inadequate; rather, the focus should be on transformation reconciled with existing institutions and the contextual meaning of justice.

3.   Constitution making and gender equality

With specific regard to the gender equality agenda in transitional justice and constitution making, contemporary scholarship started paying attention to demands for a feminist perspective only as a consequence of widespread sexual violence against female civilian populations in the Balkans conflict (see for example Allen, 1996; Askin, 1997; Copelon, 1995; Meznaric, 1994). Currently, feminist priorities in transitional justice scholarship are "(1) the recognition of gender-specific harms against women in transitional justice mechanisms and processes; (2) the amelioration of structural gender inequalities that make women particularly vulnerable to certain harms; and (3) the participation of women in the processes and institutions of transitional justice" (O'Rourke, 2015, p. 118).

Generally speaking, nationalism and war usually facilitate a cultural patriarchal backlash with regard to the role of women in society, while it is also true that women, during wartime, experience new identities and responsibilities. Moreover, "the supposed reconciliation, and oppositions to reconciliation, which must take place at the wars' end, aims to create a coherent memory and identity from a context, which is much more fragile and unstable" (Luci, 2005, p. 146).

---

5. See Chumbipuma Aguirre et al. v. State of Peru (The Barrios Altos Case) 14 May 2001, Series C No. 75 (Inter-American Court of Human Rights).

This process is relevant to the definition of what has been identified above as the constitutional self; in fact, the restoration of the *status quo ante* combined with the necessity to build a 'people' based on the identification of who 'we' is as opposed to 'the other', may cause a conundrum for gender equality in nation building, as this operation has historically excluded women (Ivekovic, 1999, p. 17)[6]. On the basis of past experience, for example in former Yugoslavia where "from a specific feminist activity, groups moved on to becoming more anti-nationalist and pacifist" (Ivekovic, 1999, p. 98), it appears to be crucial, for both international and local actors, to keep the focus on women as inspirers, recipients, and deliverers of (transitional) justice. This will ensure that women are a constituent subject and not the object of a gender-blind constituent process.

4. Transitional justice, constitution making, and gender equality: why is a human rights centered approach the best option available?

Adopting a taken-out-of-context toolkit/best practice approach to the inclusion of gender equality in constitution making, particularly if the latter follows a transitional justice process, is not advisable for a number of reasons. First of all, a toolkit approach could backfire on women in post-conflict societies. Second, especially for international and transnational organizations, it is advisable to move beyond advocacy of interest-based representation (e.g. reserved quotas) and take advantage of the jurisdictional and human rights-centered form of transitional justice, which positively focuses on context by working on individual cases. Accordingly, their action should be led by the principle of complementarity, i.e. complementing the transformative national project during the transitional justice phase. An example may clarify this final point. The deadline for victims to file cases of human rights abuses committed between July 1955 and December 2013 in front of the Tunisian Truth and Dignity Commission expired on June 15 2016. Some 46,500 cases were filed, of which 8,800 by

---

6. "Come le altre «minoranze», per esempio gli albanesi jugoslavi agli occhi dei nazionalisti serbi, o i serbi agli occhi dei nazionalisti croati, la donna avrebbe diritto alla democrazia (e, nel migliore dei casi, vi sarebbe rappresentata) solo se potesse provare la sua appartenenza alla specie umana secondo il modello maschile (o serbo, o...). Ma ciò è sempre impossibile da provare per chi, in quello stesso contesto, è ammesso solo in quanto è assente: in quel contesto che esclude".

women, i.e. nearly 21% of the total complaints. This percentage was only 5% at the beginning of the campaign and has risen significantly in the last few months thanks to the efforts of the *Association Tounissiet* (Tunisian women) and the International Center for Transitional Justice (ICTJ). The first went from door to door to find victims and persuade them to take part in the transitional justice process by filing their stories; the second trained eleven women's associations in reaching out to female victims and informing them about the urgency of filing their cases (Belhassine, 2016), thus positively impacting the transitional justice system through cooperative actions aimed at supporting and complementing the constitutionally vested body.

Moreover, it should be underlined that international transitional justice mechanisms that end up being unable to deliver justice and truth to victims may turn out to be counterproductive. For example, the "top-down agenda for transitional justice in Kosovo, focused mainly on the institutional level, has ignored truth-seeking, victim support, apologies, reparation, and community reconciliation" and has instead "resulted in unplanned outcomes fuelling ethno-nationalist discourses and increasing popular legitimacy of former combatants and their political power" (Visoka, 2016, p. 7). By side-lining civilian and minority victims of the conflict, it goes without saying that, in such a context, women who experienced and survived sexual violence were overshadowed and forgotten on one hand, and socially and politically stigmatized on the other. In order "to overcome these challenges, civil society organizations have played a vital role in recognizing the victims of conflict in Kosovo as well as filling the vacuum created by the lack of a formal truth-seeking mechanism" (Visoka, 2016, p. 71) (e.g. Kosovo Memory Book, a project of the Humanitarian Law Center).

5. Transitional justice, gender equality, and the future of Syrian women

Turning back to the conflict in Syria, when the time comes to address the genocide of the Yazidis, lessons based on the experience of the last 25 years

should be taken into account. In the report entitled *"They came to destroy":
ISIS Crimes Against the Yazidis*, released on the 16th of June 2016 (UNHRC,
2016), the Independent International Commission of Inquiry on the Syrian Arab
Republic found that many of the women and girls "were sold as chattel and
sexually enslaved by [ISIS] fighters. […] ISIS committed the crime of genocide
by seeking to destroy the Yazidis through killings, sexual slavery, enslavement,
torture, forcible displacement, the transfer of children, and measures intended to
prohibit the birth of Yazidi children" (OHCHR, n.d., para 3). A robust, human
rights-centered form of transitional justice in Syria will help form a constitutional
system that provides accountability for crimes committed by state and non-state
actors. Such a system must eschew gender-blindness and seek to include women
in all stages of peace promotion. Again, women were and still are the ones paying
the highest price in terms of suffering and human rights violations; therefore,
in my opinion, when international organizations finally start prosecuting these
heinous crimes, they should engage with civil society at a local level so as to
really make women important stakeholders in the constitution making process.

References

Allen, B. (1996). *Rape warfare: the hidden genocide in Bosnia-Herzegovina and Croatia.*
University of Minnesota Press.

Askin, K. D. (1997). *War crimes against women: prosecution in international war crimes
tribunals.* Kluwer Law International.

Belhassine, O. (2016, June 9). Women victims step up as Tunisia truth commission deadline
nears. *Justice info.net.* http://www.justiceinfo.net/en/justice-reconciliation/27798-
women-victims-step-up-as-tunisia-truth-commission-deadline-nears.html

CEDAW. (1979). UN General Assembly, Convention on the Elimination of All Forms of
Discrimination Against Women. *United Nations, Treaty Series, 1249, p. 13.* http://www.
refworld.org/docid/3ae6b3970.html

Copelon, R. (1995). *Gendered war crimes: reconceptualizing rape in time of war.* In J. Peters
& A. Wolper (Eds), *Women's rights, human rights: international feminist perspectives*
(pp. 197-214). Routledge.

Ivekovic, R. (1999). *La Balcanizzazione della Ragione.* Manifesto libri.

Luci, N. (2005). Transitions and traditions: redefining kinship, nation and gender in Kosova. *Anthropological yearbook of European cultures. Gender and Nation in South Eastern Europe, 14*, 143-169.

Meznaric, S. (1994). Gender as an ethno-marker: rape, war and identity in the former Yugoslavia. In V. M. Moghadam (Ed.), *Identity politics and women: cultural reassertion and feminisms in international perspective* (pp. 76-97). Westview Press.

OHCHR. (n.d.). *Commission of inquiry on Syria calls for justice on the occasion of the third anniversary of ISIL's attack on the Yazidis.* http://www.ohchr.org/EN/NewsEvents/Pages/DisplayNews.aspx?NewsID=21935&LangID=E

O'Rourke, C. (2013). Gender politics in transitional justice – feminist scholarship in transitional justice: a de-politicising impulse. In *Women's Studies International Forum* (vol. 51). Routledge.

O'Rourke, C. (2015). Feminist scholarship in transitional justice: a de-politicising impulse? *Women's Studies International Forum, 51*, 118-127. https://doi.org/10.1016/j.wsif.2014.11.003

Teitel, R. (2003). Theoretical and international framework: transitional justice in a new era. *Fordham International Law Journal, 26*(4), 893-906.

Teitel, R. (2014). *Transitional justice and the transformation of constitutionalism.* In T. Ginsborg & R. Dixon (Eds), *Comparative constitutional law.* Edward Elgar Publishing. https://doi.org/10.1093/acprof:oso/9780195394948.003.0011

UNHRC. (2016). *Report of the independent international commission of inquiry on the Syrian Arab Republic: "They came to destroy": ISIS Crimes Against the Yazidis*, A/HRC/32/CRP.2. http://www.ohchr.org/Documents/HRBodies/HRCouncil/CoISyria/A_HRC_32_CRP.2_en.pdf

UNHRC. (2017). *Report of the independent international commission of inquiry on the Syrian Arab Republic* A/HRC/33/55 B. https://documents-dds-ny.un.org/doc/UNDOC/GEN/G16/178/60/PDF/G1617860.pdf

Visoka, G. (2016). Arrested truth: transitional justice and the politics of ermembrance in Kosovo. *Journal of Human Rights Practice, 8*(1), 62-80. https://doi.org/10.1093/jhuman/huv017

Section 2.

The role of women in the Syrian uprising and in the political transitional process

Despite women's participation and visibility in uprisings, the greatest risk in transitional processes lies in truncated or aborted transitions where women's rights are given up as an item of populist compromise. This session explores how women's rights organisations in Syria articulated and supported women's claims for new representation and for a key role in bodies negotiating the transition towards democracy and regime change.

5 Lineages and trajectories of change and conflict in Syria

Massimiliano Trentin[1]

This chapter tries to view the current conflict in Syria from a historical and political perspective. With all the analytical limits of summaries, it highlights the main lineages of social and political conflict in the country: from the major changes that occurred in the 2000's, to the transformation of the political conflict in 2011 into a full-scale war until late 2016. It also takes a look at the main features of the political regimes that developed alongside the conflict, with a final remark on a possible post-war Syria.

1.   Lineages of development and conflict

In the well-known interview released in late January 2011 for *The Wall Street Journal*, Syrian President Bashar al-Assad stated that the on-going uprisings in Arab countries (namely Tunisia, Egypt, Bahrain, and Yemen) would not affect Syria thanks to the government and state's close relations to their people (WSJ, 2011). According to him, the primary factor cementing the alliance between the ruling elite and the Syrian population was the posture that Damascus had adopted in Arab, Middle Eastern and international affairs, namely, the 'resistance' to foreign intervention (like the West-led 'regime-change' in Iraq in 2003), diktats (like the European Union requests for the disarmament of Weapons of Mass Destruction (WMD) vs. the granting of the Association Agreement in 2009), and Israeli expansionism (occupation of the Syrian Golan Heights, the summer 2006 war against Lebanon). Second, the path of economic reforms adopted since his access to power in 2000 secured the country from major social discontent: he conceded that much was still to be done, but the country was on the 'right' path

---

1. University of Bologna, Bologna, Italy; massimiliano.trentin@unibo.it

How to cite this chapter: Trentin, M. (2018). Lineages and trajectories of change and conflict in Syria. In C. Padovani & F. Helm (Eds), *Rethinking the transition process in Syria: constitution, participation and gender equality* (pp. 73-88). Research-publishing.net. https://doi.org/10.14705/rpnet.2018.21.759

73

of change. However, he proved wrong because despite all its peculiarities, Syria was no exception to the processes of uneven development that has characterized the Arab world in recent decades and led to popular mobilization, both civic (the 'uprisings' in 2010-2012) and violent (the 'wars' in 2012-2016) (Aita, 2014, p. 21; Declich, 2017, p. 47; Van Dam, 2017, p. 64).

A few months later, in March 2011, the country spiralled into a full-scale crisis, where popular demonstrations for civic and political reforms were met by the 'regime' (*al-nizam)* with a mix of coercion, implemented through the large array of security services (*al-mukhabarat*) and elite units of the Syrian armed forces (Republican Guard), and a set of political reforms meant to appease dissent without endangering the primacy of the existing ruling elite (April, 2012). However, the 'traditional' strategy did not work in front of quite 'new' actors on the ground. Both the massive display of violence against mostly non-violent activists and the gathering of international support for the opposition soon turned the confrontation into open, armed conflict, where all parties believed they were fighting an 'existential' threat and thus behaved along the 'winner-takes-all' strategy. From early 2012, Syria was engulfed in a conflict that was at once civil, regional, and international, with multiple actors moving into the battlefield in order to grasp the economic and political assets enshrined in the lands and the people of modern Syria.

Most of the literature on the conflict has highlighted its changing nature. First, it was a confrontation between a broad set of social groups that were largely marginalized by the ruling elites, particularly during the 2000's, and a 'regime' which struggled to maintain its monopoly over the state and politics while disbanding those institutions and policies that so far had guaranteed its social constituencies. The geography of early demonstrations largely coincided with those urban centers in rural provinces (Deraa, Homs, Hama, Idlib, Deir al-Zor) that had been excluded from development policies or the inflow of private wealth that swept across Syria along the decade prior to the war (Al Laithy & Abu-Islamil, 2005, pp. 27, 35; Sayigh, 2016; SCPR, 2013, p. 21). With the notable exception of the Mediterranean coast, these provinces were the bulwark of the Baathist social constituencies: the latter's leadership being largely of rural, provincial origin, ascended to power through the development of state institutions (armed forces, security services, education, health, and agricultural cooperatives) and mass organizations (Ba'th Party and Labour Unions) (Balanche, 2006; Batatu, 1999). The fiscal crisis of the state and the 'austerity' measures of the 1980's, the limited liberalizations of the 1990's, and the major push towards private sector- and market-based reforms shifted the regime's privileged constituencies from the rural, popular ones, to the urban, wealthy ones (Haddad, 2012).

The delicate balance between those institutions that represented the different social and political constituencies under the long, embattled presidency of Hafez al-Assad was put under heavy strain by the reforms enforced by his son Bashar from the mid-2000's. Once appointed to the presidency in 2000, he raised hopes for a relaxation of the Ba'thist monopoly on politics, but the repression of the civic, urban movement of the 'Damascus Spring' in 2001 signalled the limits on the scope of any reform process (Wieland, 2012, pp. 46-48): this latter might concern first and foremost economics, and met the approval of the elite in order to consolidate rather than endanger the current pillars of the state, namely the presidency and the security forces. The external threat of the US-led 'regime-change' in Iraq in 2003, and rising pressure from European states against Damascus to relinquish its political control over neighboring Lebanon in 2005, contributed to distancing the 'regime' from the West and aligning it to more secure and traditional allies, like Iran, Russia, and China, which did not question the connections between domestic politics, development, and international relations (Zorob, 2007). While engineering new waves of political co-optation for private entrepreneurs and religious leaders, major space was accorded to wealthy businessmen in order to mobilize private capital in those sectors that were deemed more rewarding in terms of profits. During the 2000's, the economic sectors that mostly contributed to the growth of the Gross Domestic Product (GDP) were energy, trade, transport, information-technologies, finance, tourism, and real estate. Instead, agriculture, industry, and manufacturing, long being the backbone of the Ba'thist-led agro-industrial development, suffered from de facto de-investment in infrastructure, like irrigation systems (Mohtadi, 2012). The public (state and cooperatives) abstained for fiscal reasons, and the private focused on short-term production for export, thanks to the differentials between the subsidized costs of production (originally meant for domestic consumption) and the neighboring countries' market prices.

With all due peculiarities in time and space, Syria embarked on a process of development which coupled the basics of 'accumulation by dispossession', which featured other cases in neoliberal globalization, with the so called 'Dubai Consensus', which translated the supply-based, market-oriented 'Washington Consensus' of the 1990's into the Arab world of the 2000's (Hanieh, 2011; Harvey, 2003, p. 137).

Income, as well as the polarization of living conditions, increased sharply between provinces, to the detriment of waged-labor, peasant and urban, small merchants. The Regional Congress of the Ba'th Party in 2005 adopted the 'Social-Market Economy' model in the Tenth Five-Year Plan, which officially recognized the private sector as the main engine for growth and employment, whereas the public would guarantee social cohesion by providing basic services to those left out by market competition (SAR, 2016). However, there was no major fund left for the 'social' (Abboud, 2015) once the Plan was implemented, and private actors, both domestic and foreign, mostly preferred to invest in economic activities which guaranteed short-term profits but did not provide major employment at a critical conjuncture, namely when Syria was experiencing the massive entry of the 'baby-boomers' of the 1980's and 1990's into the labor-market (Aita, 2011). In their twenties and thirties, quite well-educated and highly connected to the rest of the world by the widespread and skilful use of information technologies, the new generations were unable to find any employment suited to their competences and life-expectations, if any at all, and were largely prevented from expressing their opinions in public, least of all organizing and engaging in politics, apart from in the regime's institutions.

Discontent and dissent found space on the internet, while resilience, 'quiet encroachment', and sporadic riots were devied as a major strategy for living as in other Arab states (Bayat, 2010, p. 43; Chalcraft, 2016, p. 22). Moreover, the dismantling of infrastructure and services in rural areas accelerated the peasants' exodus towards urban centers. While Damascus and Aleppo, the main 'global cities' of Syria, still managed the process, this was not the case for provincial centers excluded from the new patterns of development and the related new geography of wealth and power: in particular, this was the case of the rural, impoverished North-east (Ababsa, 2015). Religious groups and institutions like mosques, churches, and charitable associations were granted more space as service suppliers in order to counterbalance the retreat of state institutions in the peripheral areas (Aita, 2013; De Elvira & Zintl, 2012). In this case, the Presidency and security services cultivated close relations with specific religious forces as long as they promoted regime policies and prevented the emergence of any organized dissent: like co-opting conservatives, leading 'ulama in Damascus or Aleppo, and flirting with radical, Salafi ones against US forces in Iraq (Lister, 2015, p. 31; Mubayed, 2015, p. 42; Pierret, 2011; Weiss & Hassan, 2015, p. 99). However, once the regime faced crisis, these forces proved their autonomy and popular support.

In all cases, the presidency, the security forces, and small groups of wealthy businessmen became the backbone of the 'authoritarian upgrading' of the Syrian regime, whereas mass organizations, like the Ba'th Party, the Unions, and the state, were downgraded to a secondary role (Hinnebusch, 2012; Trombetta, 2014). Given this trend, the security services, and their practices of coercion and corruption, became the main interface of the regime for people living in the restive, subaltern suburbs of Damascus and Aleppo, as well as in rural provinces (Glasman, 2013).

Social polarization, discontent, and early signs of tensions led the Presidency to a partial reassessment of the economic policies in 2010: the next XI Five-Year Plan was to focus back on agriculture and manufacturing, as well as on state intervention in the economy and the provision of social services (Amonajed, 2012; Syria Today, 2010). And yet, while liberalization was still deemed necessary to trigger domestic growth, there were few signs for tackling the so-called 'institutional bottlenecks' that prevented the development of any 'liberal' context in Syria. This was coupled with the engagement of former leading figures of the Ba'thist leadership who had been side-lined previously and were known both for their links to provincial Syria and security-oriented approach to dissent (Abbas, 2011). The move was significant insofar as it meant that the Syrian leadership was preparing for major challenges ahead, given the growing instability in other Arab countries.

2.   From political to armed conflict

The chronicles of the early protests accounted for their 'civic' features: namely, ultimate opposition to the police and security forces' arbitrariness in enforcing law, their brutality in repressing dissent, and eventually their unaccountability to ordinary citizens. The regime resorted to the traditional strategy of hitting the frontline of dissent hard with violent coercion while co-opting the latter's constituencies with limited rewards. Though that had worked on previous occasions, this time protesters engaged in sustained struggle, banking on the mobilization of Arab and foreign support to put pressure on Damascus, as they thought had occurred in Tunisia, Egypt, and later on Libya. The increasing, massive use of military violence by the elite units of the Syrian armed forces against protesters and the latter's resort first to non-violence and later to armed force led to an escalation of the crisis, whose main trajectories might be summarized as follows, with all due limits[2].

Between early 2011 and early 2012, the confrontation was primarily between Syrian actors (Declich, 2017, p. 89; Phillips, 2016, p. 40; Van Dam, 2017, p. 96). On the opposition side, forces developed along the axis of 'moderate-to-radical' reform of the 'regime'. However, the escalation of violence led to an outright rejection of the 'regime' as a whole, though without elaborating precisely whether the latter meant the whole 'state' or just the removal of the ruling elite. On the government side, after a referendum on February 2012, a new Constitution was adopted whose reforms were nevertheless deemed 'too little, too late'. Activists scattered around the country organized into the Local Coordination Committees, while defectors from the Syrian Army formed the 'Free Syrian Army' (FSA), and increasingly relied on foreign powers for political and logistical support,

---

2. For a timeline of the crisis in Syria, see the British guardian.co.uk for an accurate interactive map, https://www. theguardian.com/world/interactive/2012/feb/15/syria-timeline-how-conflict-escalated-interactive.

especially Turkey, the Gulf states, and NATO countries (later to be named 'The Friends of Syria'). The Arab Gulf monarchies planned to get rid of al Assad and the Ba'thists namely, difficult partners and long-standing allies of their Iranian rival. In parallel, the presidency in Damascus was confident of its major allies' support (Iran and Russia) and continued with the 'hard-stick' and 'small-carrot' strategy. The United Nations (UN) tried to mediate by sponsoring talks and meetings between parties (Geneva I, June 2012).

From mid-2012 to summer 2013, with strong foreign backing from NATO countries as well, the opposition conquered and managed territories in provincial Syria, and moved military confrontation into the main urban centers. Radical, jihadist movements entered the conflict and proved skilful in waging war, enforcing discipline on armed units, channelling funds from abroad, and providing services to the areas under their control. Kurdish forces in the north began to act in their native territories against the FSA, jihadis (battles of Ras al-'Ayn, 2012-2013), and occasionally against the Syrian armed forces, whereas the latter grew over-stretched in personnel and retreated to defend 'core' areas from Damascus to the Mediterranean coast.

The refusal by the US and UK to take military action against al Assad in the event of the chemical attacks in Damascus in August 2013 pushed the Lebanese militia of Hezbollah and Iran to engage officially, and help the Syrian armed forces to reconquer strategic areas in the center-west of the country throughout 2014. In the opposition camp, space was open for radical, jihadi forces with sectarian discourse and agendas to take the lead in the armed struggle against the regime and the establishment of emirates or radical, Salafi systems of governance: especially in the Idlib province around Damascus and in eastern Syria along the Euphrates river. However, they split into different factions as soon as the so-called Islamic State in Iraq and the Levant ('Islamic State' (IS), by June 2014) moved from neighboring Iraq to assert its primacy over Syrian rebels. Kurdish forces in the north resisted against the IS and, after the battle of Kobane/'Ayn al 'Arab (2014), consolidated their project for an autonomous municipal confederation ('Rojava'). UN-backed talks (Geneva II, January-February 2014) stalled as all parties tried to set 'facts on the ground' to their favor[3]. Supported by Turkey and the Gulf monarchies, rebels gathered forces around Islamist groups and fought back against the government in the north and south from early 2015 in a last bid for regime-reversal. Damascus was under heavy strain for lack of combat personnel and lack of discipline among pro-regime militias – National Defence Forces (NDF) – and Iranian-trained forces.

Russia intervened directly in September 2015 with a heavy air campaign, officially against the 'terrorist' forces of the IS, but substantially against al-Qaeda in Syria (Jabhat al-Nusra) and all other rebel forces (FSA) which posed a major threat to the strategic 'core' of the regime. By reversing the military balance on the ground, Moscow planned to force rebels and their foreign backers to a 'political solution' based upon the primacy of existing state institutions, especially the regular Syrian armed forces. Meanwhile, Western countries (especially, the US, France, and the UK) began reassessing their involvement in Syria (logistics, training, funds) after the 'nuclear deal' with Iran in July 2015, which paved the way to a major appeasement in mutual relationships, and a de facto concerted campaign against the IS in Iraq.

During 2016, previous processes were consolidated. Thanks to renewed military and organizational support from Russia, Damascus slowly took back control of more territory, both through military conquests and 'siege' strategies, until the major battle for Aleppo in late 2016. The rebels staged repeated counter-offensives in the north and Aleppo, which proved effective but short-lived because of diminished foreign support. Meanwhile, with US support and Russian acquiescence, Kurdish-led forces – the Syrian Democratic Forces (SDF) – expanded their reach against the IS in the north, liberating the city of Manbij, on the west bank of the Euphrates river, and laying siege to Raqqa, the de facto capital of the IS in Syria; in turn, this prompted Turkey's military intervention beyond its border with Syria in October 2016. The end of the fifth year of war and 2017 accounted for the total conquest of Aleppo city by the Syrian Army and its allies and the ejection of the rebels from most of the western parts of Syria under the UN-backed and Russian-led 'de-escalation zones'; the rebel containment in

---

3. For a timeline of UN-based diplomatic activities in Syria, see the website of Security Council Report, http://www.securitycouncilreport.org/chronology/syria.php.

the Idlib province, where jihadis made their bid for leadership; the retreat of the IS down to the Euphrates river in the east and out of all major urban centers, from Raqqa to Deir er Zur and Albu Kamal; the consolidation of Kurdish-led 'Rojava'; and last but not least, the contest for leadership in the southern and eastern provinces between Western, Gulf-backed rebels and government forces.

3. Back to the future: from war to political, civic conflict?

The dynamics of the conflict in Syria have proven that, on their own, neither the Syrian government nor the opposition had the decisive capacity to strike a fatal blow against the other and win the conflict by military means. A strategic stalemate soon translated into a war of attrition. The so-called 'regime' proved more cohesive than expected, it had long experience in political survival and diplomacy, it could count on the asset of the remaining state institutions, and held major firepower but lacked sufficient human resources for waging a long war (Holliday, 2013; Kozak, 2015). The opposition enjoyed significant popular and international support and was rich and creative in establishing alternative patterns of governance and development (from the Local Coordination Committees to the Kurdish-led Rojava), even in war-contexts. However it suffered from scarce resources and deep fragmentation: besides sharing a common stance against the government in Damascus, they differed in the sources of political legitimacy (religion, sectarianism, nationalism, communitarianism) and related discourse, as well as in the negotiating strategies, which undermined their efficacy in crucial moments, and even led to armed clashes (Caffarella & Casagrande, 2015; Hassan, 2012; Holliday, 2012; Sayigh, 2013).

Both camps had to rely increasingly on foreign support for diplomacy, finance, logistics, and armament supply. Despite frictions on military strategies, namely the role of militias, Iran and Russia proved more cohesive and coherent in their support to the Syrian regime, which eventually proved decisive to tilt the strategic balance of forces in their favor in late 2013 and 2015. On the contrary, NATO and Gulf monarchies' support proved limited, hesitant, and contradictory, providing aid to competing, rival groups with divergent projects for political and social development (Caffarella & Casagrande, 2016; Phillips, 2016, pp. 59, 147, 168; Van Dam, 2017, p. 119). Last but not least, though very much dependent, the Syrian government still enjoyed quite a leverage vis-à-vis Moscow and Tehran in order to set its own priorities; on the contrary, the opposition had quite a limited influence over its foreign backers, and followed rather than conditioned their priorities.

Despite the strategic stalemate, until late 2016 both the regime and the opposition framed their priorities and discourses along the patterns of a zero-sum game: accordingly, the 'other' represented not just a political rival but an existential, physical threat, with whom no legitimate compromise might be struck except for surrender and total, unconditional defeat. The Syrian government labelled all rebel factions as 'terrorists' and 'foreigners' whereas the latter denigrated Damascus as the 'regime', 'killers', 'unbelievers' (targeting the 'Alawite or Shia' members), or simply in the hands of the 'Persians' (meaning, Iran). Given the social fabrics of Syria, such uncompromising positions easily translated into the ideological categories and discourse of sectarianism, which flattens the complexity of affiliations and 'multiple identities' into just one binary category, as promoted by radical forces inside both camps (Hinnebusch, 2016).

The widespread, direct experience of mass violence, death, and destruction pushed individuals and groups 'to close ranks' to the community they thought would guarantee their physical safety and material survival which, in the Syrian context, might coincide with ethnic and sectarian groups. Evidence from the ground shows the shifting nature of divisions: first, the divide between pro/ against the regime cut cross Syrian society; then, as the political conflict turned into an armed one, it located to specific territories (provinces, municipalities, districts) (Pierret, 2012; Rey, 2013, p. 89) whose social composition grew more homogeneous due to migrations and forced displacements; from then on, sectarianism was able to develop as a framework for defensive and offensive action, with substantial support from foreign countries as well (The Day After, 2016; Wherey, 2013). This process undermined any unitary projects or institutions.

A major consequence of such uncompromising postures concerned the central state institutions: since the 'regime' in Damascus kept control over most of them, their legitimacy as pillars of common affiliation and citizenship has been further discredited in the eyes of the opposition and their popular constituencies. All this, despite the fact that at the beginning most of the claims concerned not the value of the 'state' per se, but its reform and relinquishing from the control of the ruling elite (Aita, 2013, pp. 92-95).

As the armed conflict was prolonged, different sets of government developed in the war-torn Syria: a military-led, political regime under the capital Damascus where the state decentralized most services to local levels but prevented popular participation in the decision-making process (SCPR, 2016a; Yazighi, 2014); radical Islamist-led regimes, under the IS or other jihadi forces, where minimal government institutions were built or run along supposedly Islamist criteria and popular participation was either prevented or limited to the norms set by the central leadership (Rey, 2017, p. 33); the Kurdish-led Rojava as well as other experiments in opposition-held territories saw citizens step in to run basic, public services according to their professional competence, and participated in the political decision-making process (Federici, 2015, pp. 81-90); here, a major difference concerned the capacity to provide physical security by centralizing or coordinating armed groups.

Along the ups and downs of the conflict, several actors elaborated and submitted different political solutions to the crisis: from the regime to the opposition groups, from foreign powers to the UN, there was considerable consensus on the fact that a political solution would prevent further destruction and civil suffering. However, all efforts at negotiations, like the UN-sponsored 'Geneva talks', stalled on the issue of the role of President Bashar al-Assad and his loyal majors in any 'political transition'. Both Damascus and jihadi-led rebels entrenched uncompromising stances, banking on their respective 'long-term' resistance capacity: as a consequence, time has never been 'ripe' for real negotiations and conflict resolution (Van Dam, 2017, p. 138; Zartmann, 2008). Then, since 2015, Russian proposals were limited to 'enlarging' the current regime to some opposition groups, thus reflecting the new military balance on the ground.

From 2016 Damascus banked on military success to enforce only 'local' deals where rebels surrender, give up weapons, and migrate to other opposition-held territories.

By December 2016, the death toll was estimated to be 500,000 people. Over 4.8 million have fled the country, mostly to neighboring Turkey, Lebanon, and Jordan, and 6.3 million are internally displaced. Thirteen and a half million need humanitarian assistance, and less than a half is actually met by domestic and foreign assistance[4]. The agricultural, industrial, and infrastructural capacity of Syria has been cut to one-third, downgrading the country to a "shattered, fragmented" war economy, "mainly dominated by subjugating powers" and "dependent on external support" (SCPR, 2016a, pp. 23-26; SCPR, 2016b, pp. 12-38; UN ESCWA, 2016a, pp. 83-87). Millions of children have lost years of school learning, and illiteracy has come back to Syria as a mass phenomenon. Research institutions and UN agencies have estimated that Syria would need at least twenty-five years to recover from the war. However, only a "new social contract" and new development paradigms might grant Syrian citizens the chance for effective participation in the reconstruction process, as well as for sustainable development (UN ESCWA, 2016a, pp. 8, 43).

Within such a disastrous context, projects for the reconstruction of Syria have begun to move since 2015. The country has experienced years of de facto partition, with different political and economic regimes at work. Nevertheless, connections throughout territories have held for basic items like energy, currency, salaries for public employees and, albeit sketchy, transport as well. The process of reconstruction might be an opportunity to rebuild the country's social and political community, which would have to be different from the past because of the radical experience people have lived through. As other cases have shown, 'institutions' might play a decisive role in the process, and the state in particular. Despite the latter's disruption, all major forces in Syria still defend the territorial and political unity of the country, countering all projects for partition into small, ethno-sectarian statelets (like, IS caliphates, jihadi 'emirates', or foreign

---

4. See statistics from UN Office for the Coordination of Humanitarian Affairs, www.unocha.org/syria.

protectorates). Indeed, the struggle still concerns the kind of political regime and state institutions to develop in Syria. With all limits due to warfare and scarcity, there have been plenty of experiences of self-government by local communities: here, people learned to master common goods by enhancing their capabilities and competences.

Given the massive scale of destruction and fiscal distress of the Syrian central state, it is hardly possible that the latter, in its current shape, could work as the main driver for reconstruction and development as has occurred in previous crises. For all these contingent and structural reasons, the decentralization of state institutions, both political and administrative, based on the specifics of territories and reconstruction needs, might provide a useful framework to match the unity of the country with the enhancement of people's competences at different levels: municipal, provincial, and national (Harb & Atallah, 2015). At all levels and for most actors involved, the participation of women has been so far of primary importance: not only as for care-work but as primary, frontline agents of political mobilization and construction of different patterns of government, both conservative and progressive ones. Such an experience will not be easily marginalized in any credible, post-war reconstruction effort. However, such potential cannot be detached from the adoption of new paradigms of economic development that equally enhance popular participation in the decision-making process, which is far from obvious given the previous record of international agencies and foreign advice (Abu Mosleh, 2014; SCPR, 2016b, pp. 81-88; UN ESCWA, 2016b). Far from giving a chance to secession and sectarianism in Syria, this framework might couple the resilience of citizens' participation in development with the endurance of state institutions.

References

Ababsa, M. (2015). The end of a world. Drought and agrarian transformation. In R. Hinnebusch & T. Zintl (Eds), *From reform to revolt. Political economy and international relations* (pp. 199-223). Syracuse University Press.

Abbas, H. (2011). The dynamics of the uprisings in Syria. *Arab Reform Brief, 51*, 1-10.

Abboud, S. N. (2015). Locating the social in the social market economy. In R. Hinnebusch & T. Zintl (Eds), *From reform to revolt. Political economy and international relations* (pp. 45-65). Syracuse University Press.

Abu Mosleh, F. (2014, September 11). The Lebanese model for the reconstruction of Syria: the ESCWA bid to hold Syria hostage to debt. *Al-Akhbar.*

Aita, S. (2011). *Les travailleurs arabes hors-la-loi. Emploi et droit de travail dans les Pays arabes de la Méditerranée.* L'Harmattan.

Aita, S. (2013). Nuovi e vecchi conflitti nella Siria della rivoluzione. *Afriche e Orienti, 1*(2), 89-101.

Aita, S. (2014). Le ragioni economiche e sociali delle rivolte arabe. In L. Paggi (Ed.), *Le rivolte arabe e le repliche della storia.* Ombre Corte.

Al Laithy, R., & Abu-Islamil, K. (2005). *Poverty in Syria, 1996-2004.* UNDP.

Amonajed. (2012). *The future of Syrian industry iunder the eleventh five year plan 2011-2015.* Syrian Center for Political and Strategic Studies.

Balanche, F. (2006). *La région alaouites et le pouvoir syrien.* Khartala.

Batatu, H. (1999). *Syria's peasantry, the descendants of its lesser rural notables, and their politics.* Princeton University Press.

Bayat, A. (2010). *Life as politics. How ordinary people changed the Middle East.* Stanford University Press.

Caffarella, J., & Casagrande, G. (2015). *Syrian opposition guide.* Institute for the Study of War.

Caffarella, J., & Casagrande, G. (2016). *Syrian armed opposition powerbrokers.* Institute for the Study of War.

Chalcraft, J. (2016). *Popular politics in the making of the modern Middle East.* Cambridge University Press. https://doi.org/10.1017/CBO9780511843952

De Elvira, L. R., & Zintl, T. (2012). *Civil society and the State in Syria: the outsourcing of social responsibility.* St Andrews Papers on Contemporary Syria. Lynne Rienner.

Declich, L. (2017). *Siria, la rivoluzione rimossa. Dalla rivolta del 2011 alla Guerra.* Alegre.

Federici, V. (2015). The rise of Rojava: Kurdish autonomy in the Syrian conflict. *SAIS Review of International Affairs, 35*(2), 81-90

Glasman, W. (2013). Les ressources sécuritaires du regime. In F. Burgat & B. Paoli (Eds), *Pas de Printemps pour la Syrie. Les clés pour comprendre les acteurs et les défis de la crise* (pp. 33-54). La Découverte.

Haddad, B. (2012). *Business network in Syria. The political economy of authoritarian resilience.* Stanford University Press.

Hanieh, A. (2011). *Capitalism and class in Gulf Arab States.* Palgrave MacMillan. https://doi. org/10.1057/9780230119604

Harb, M., & Atallah, S. (2015). *Local governments and public goods: assessing decentralization in the Arab World.* Lebanese Center for Policy Studies.

Harvey, D. (2003). *The new imperialism.* Oxford University Press.

Hassan, H. (2012). *Syria's local leadership.* Analysis on Arab Reform, Sada.

Hinnebusch, R. (2012). Syria: from authoritarian upgrading to revolution? *International Affairs, 88,* 95-113.

Hinnebusch, R. (2016). *The sectarian revolution in the Middle East, revolutions: global trends and regional issues, 4*(1), 120-152.

Holliday, J. (2012). *Syria's maturing insurgency.* Institute for the Study of War.

Holliday, J. (2013). *The Syrian army. Doctrinal order of battle.* Institute for the Study of War.

Kozak, C. (2015). *An army in all cornerns. Assad's campaign strategy in Syria. Middle East Security Report,* n. 26. Institute for the Study of War.

Lister, C. (2015). *The Syrian Jihad. Al Qaeda, the Islamic State and the evolution of an insurgency.* Hurst.

Mohtadi, S. (2012). *Climate change and the Syrian uprising.* Bulletin of the Atomic Scientists.

Mubayed, S. (2015). *Under the Black Flag. At the frontier of the New Jihad.* I.B. Tauris.

Phillips, C. (2016). *The battle for Syria. International rivalry in the New Middle East.* Yale University Press.

Pierret, T. (2011). *Baas et Islam en Syrie. La dynastie Assad face aux oulémas.* Presses Universitaires de France.

Pierret, T. (2012). The role of the mosque in the Syrian revolt. *Near East Quarterly.*

Rey, M. (2013). La revolte des quarters: territorialisation plutot que confessionalisation. In F. Burgat & B. Paoli (Eds), *Pas de printemps pour la Syrie. Les clés pour comprendre les acteurs et les défis de la crise* (pp. 84-91). La Découverte.

Rey, M. (2017). Dall'Iraq al Medio Oriente: l'IS e la creazione di una nuova entità politica. In M. Trentin (Ed.), *L'ultimo Califfato. L'Organizzazione dello stato islamico in Medio Oriente* (pp. 33-54). Il Mulino.

SAR. (2016). *Prime Minister Office, Planning and International Cooperation Commission, Highlights of the Syrian Economy and the Tenth 5YP Strategy.* Syrian Arab Republic. http://www.planning.gov.sy/SD08/msf/1292968335_Syrian_Economy.pdf

Sayigh, Y. (2013). *The Syrian opposition's leadership problem. The Carnegie Papers.* Carnegie Endowment for International Peace.

Sayigh, Y. (2016). Who made the Arab Spring into an Arab crisis? *Al Jazeera*.

SCPR. (2013). *Socio-economic roots and the impact of the Syrian crisis. Alienation and Violence Report*. Syrian Center for Policy Research.

SCPR. (2016a). *Syria. Confronting fragmentation. Impact of Syrian Crisis Report*. Syrian Center for Policy Research.

SCPR. (2016b). *Forced dispersion. A demographic report on human status in Syria*. Syrian Center for Policy Research.

Syria Today. (2010). *Tenth five-year plan failed to meet goals, economic forum hears*.

The Day After. (2016). *Sectarianism in Syria: Survey Study*.

Trombetta, L. (2014). Beyond the party: the shifting structure of Syria's power. In L. Anceschi, G. Gervasio, & A. Teti (Eds), *Hidden geographies: informal powers in the Greater Middle East* (pp. 24-40). Routledge.

UN ESCWA. (2016a). *Survey of economic and social developments in the Arab region, 2015-2016*. UN Economic and Social Commission for Western Asia.

UN ESCWA. (2016b). *Administrative governance and decentralization. The national agenda for the future of Syria*. UN Economic and Social Commission for Western Asia.

Van Dam, N. (2017). *Destroying the Nation. The Civil War in Syria*, I.B. Tauris.

Weiss, M., & Hassan, H. (2015). *ISIS. Inside the army of terror*. Ergan Arts.

Wherey, F. (2013). *Syria's sectarian ripples across the Gulf*. Peace Brief n. 161. United States Institute of Peace.

Wieland, C. (2012). *A decade of lost chances. Repression and revolution from Damascus to Arab Spring*. Cune Press.

WSJ. (2011, January 31). *Interview with President Bashar al-Assad*. The Wall Street Journal. https://www.wsj.com/articles/SB10001424052748703833204576114712441122894

Yazighi, J. (2014). *Syria's war economy*. Brief Policy n. 97. European Council on Foreign Relations.

Zartmann, W. (2008). *Ripeness: the importance of timing in negotiations and conflict resolution*. E-International Relations.

Zorob, A. (2007). The potential of regional integration agreements (RIAs) in enhancing the credibility of reform: the case of the Syrian-European association agreement. *GIGA Papers, 51*.

6 Women in uprising and transitional processes: an introductory note

Annalisa Oboe[1]

During uprisings, revolutions and times of conflict, women always walk a very thin tightrope between empowerment and disempowerment; they are forced into positions of responsibility that only the day before were unthinkable and they take up leading roles to guarantee social survival and the future, but this does not guarantee that once the 'revolution' is over, their new power will be acknowledged.

Times of upheaval can be times of hope, but also of death, destruction, and mourning, in which rights are suspended and old rules are broken. These times are in all senses 'exceptional' times. When they eventually come to an end and some sort of new 'order' is established, women's participation in bringing about that newness tends to be overlooked, to be seen as 'exceptional' as the times that produced it, as extra-ordinary, anomalous. From there, the step to the restoration of old roles for women and to disempowerment is very short, and so women need to start re-negotiating again, to denounce the complicity between the post-conflict present and the status quo and re-organize a vindication of rights and status.

I want to focus briefly on the meaning of this tightrope, this crucial empowerment/ disempowerment dialectics in historical moments of political transition for women, during and after uprisings and wars, by referring to one historical experience that I have followed closely, and that has come back to me in the

1. University of Padova, Padova, Italy; annalisa.oboe@unipd.it

How to cite this chapter: Oboe, A. (2018). Women in uprising and transitional processes: an introductory note. In C. Padovani & F. Helm (Eds), *Rethinking the transition process in Syria: constitution, participation and gender equality* (pp. 89-94). Research-publishing.net. https://doi.org/10.14705/rpnet.2018.21.760

form of questions for today's work. The great event is the South African Truth and Reconciliation Commission (TRC) of the late 1990s[2].

Years ago I worked on the testimonies of the South African women who stood before the Human Rights Violation Committee during the TRC's special hearings that were held in Johannesburg on the 28th and 29th of July 1997[3]. Hundreds of victims testified, above all women, and what was striking about these women's testimonials was that they were able to disclose what had happened to family or community members but were reluctant to talk about what had happened to them. Special hearings were thus organized to encourage women to discuss their life experiences as women under apartheid. They were called upon "to speak as actors, as active participants and direct survivors of the violation of human rights […] as themselves, those that directly suffered" (Mtintso, 1997). A representative of the Federation of Transvaal Women highlighted how women in South Africa "deserve to be counted among those who have played a role. Not as wives, not as mothers, but as women, but as citizens of this country and as leaders" (Makoyane, 1997). The emphasis was clearly on recovering the women's perspectives and their roles, not only as victims but also as social actors. The hearings allowed for the various degrees to which women's identity was cancelled to come to light: from intimidation and forms of psychological pressure to annihilation through violence and torture.

Sheila Masote, daughter of the late Zeph Mothopeng, President of the Pan African Congress from 1986 to 1990, strayed from the expectations of the Committee, which had been appointed to hear about 'gross' violations of human rights, when she took the stage and vindicated her own negated self:

---

2. As explained in Oboe (2007), "[t]he South African Truth and Reconciliation Commission was called into existence in July 1995, after intensive negotiations between the African National Congress (ANC) and the National Party (NP). The mandate of the TRC was enormous: it was required to establish as complete a picture as possible of the causes, nature and extent of the gross violations of human rights which were committed during the period from 1 March 1960 to 10 May 1994; it was asked to suggest ways of repairing past wrongs and, under certain conditions, it was allowed to grant amnesty to apartheid perpetrators. In order to achieve these ambitious tasks, three committees were put into place: the Committee on Human Rights Violations (HRVC), which held public hearings where people could testify about past abuses; the Amnesty Committee, which considered applications for amnesty; and the Committee on Reparation and Rehabilitation, which recommended policies to the government regarding reparations for the victims of apartheid" (p. 72).

3. TRC Women's Hearings: http://www.justice.gov.za/trc/special/#wh

"On the programme it says I'm here to speak about – on behalf of the family. No, that is not what I am here about. [… Y]es, I'm part of the family, but I refuse to be family and have no identity as Sheila. The problem that I have always suffered and I have always said to myself is that I don't seem to be having an identity like belonging to me. I'm always either Zef's daughter, Mathopeng's daughter or Mike Masote's wife. Or no, Masote's mother and Zef Masote's mother. But no, I feel I am me. And this is why I am here" (Masote, 1997).

We gather from her stand that the TRC, alongside post-apartheid South Africa, was hardly able to offer women a proper forum, and that what it expected of them did not really coincide with what women wished or needed – new identities, new roles, new rights, which not even one of the most enlightened constitutions in the world could guarantee, unless culture changed. As stated in Oboe (2007),

"[d]espite the framing of equality and sympathy, which was at the core of the TRC, forms of social, cultural and gender inequality did get into the proceedings, which were uneasily located between past horrors and present dreams of reconciliation and justice. The women's voices came out as quite ex-centric in relation to both" (p. 63).

The questions that this reference to the TRC women's hearings triggers for me are the following: is it possible to spell out the ways in which a gendered culture may be formed, or has formed in Syria?

What is the process that will lead the majority of Syrian women to be 'themselves' rather than someone's daughter/wife/mother? I am asking this because taking away women's rights, identities, and presences is still a widespread occurrence in our unbalanced word, and we need to be watchful.

A relevant example is the predicament of women candidates during the Palestinian municipal elections of 2016, announced on the 23rd of June 2016, and repeatedly suspended (Ma'an News Agency, 2016). These were to be the first elections in all of the Palestinian territories since Hamas' takeover of the Gaza Strip in

2007. In the fraught process leading up to the vote, the exclusion of female candidates' names from campaign materials ahead of municipal elections in the West Bank and Gaza sparked a new focus on women's civil rights in Palestinian society. In some areas, women could only register and appear as candidates in the election lists as the sister/wife/daughter of some brother/husband/father, and their face could not be shown, no picture exhibited. However, the fact did not go unnoticed. News that election materials from villages near Hebron and Jenin excluded women's names (MEMO, 2016) caused an outcry on social media, birthing the Arabic hashtag "Our names should not be covered"[4]. Women took to Twitter and Facebook using the hashtag to say they were proud to put their names to their achievements, as well as those of their mothers, sisters, and daughters (McKernan, 2016). Apparently, many men did the same. The incident resonated with Palestinians, and the Central Election Commission said that the papers in question were illegal, since women are entitled to full political participation under Palestinian law.

I do not wish to conflate Syria and Palestine, but stress that patriarchy takes many forms, some more vicious than others – it may take away the subaltern woman's name and the subaltern woman's face exactly when some speaking position is apparently achieved or allowed.

One last reflection: thinking about the role of women in the Syrian uprising has made me go back to the meanings and the shapes of women's culture in relation to religion and nation.

Do you remember the scene in *The Battle of Algiers* (DZ/I 1966, dir. Gillo Pontecorvo) which is taken up as an echo in *Frantz Fanon: Black Skin, White Mask* (UK 1996, dir. Isaac Julien)? A veiled woman in Algiers, during the late '50s, in the years that saw the confrontation between Algerians and the occupying French colonial power, smuggles a gun through a French checkpoint, and she then hands it over to a member of the French Front de Libération Nationale (FLN) who kills a colonial official at a coffee table in the centre

---

4. https://goo.gl/JQ4y3B

of town. *The Battle of Algiers* reflects Fanon's arguments about the veil and violence as a justified means of anti-colonial struggle in quite a complementary way, while Julien's film takes a more critical stance towards both issues.

In the case of the veil, Pontecorvo is following Fanon's example, stressing its significance related to cultural independence from the French occupier. Accordingly, in another scene of the film, while the female FLN members prepare for the guerilla bomb attack they will carry out in the French quarter, they look uncomfortable taking off their veil and transforming their appearance into a Western one. It does not seem to be a pleasant or emancipatory act for them, as the French/Western discourse would argue. Maintaining their cultural heritage is represented as a virtue, and the veil as not oppressive, because they are shown as equal to and respected by the male FLN members.

In the film *Frantz Fanon: Black Skin, White Mask* the appropriation of the veil as a tool to hide and transport weapons and explosives is shown by means of a quotation from *The Battle of Algiers*. In both films, thereby, a critique against the Eurocentric perspective on the Muslim woman as obedient and passive is deconstructed. To Stuart Hall, who serves as a commentator in Julien's film, the women serving the FLN 'could turn the veil against its meaning'. Still, Julien uses the mentioned scene of transformation from veiled to unveiled from *The Battle of Algiers* in order to criticize Fanon's and the film's concept of the veil.

So my third and last question would be: What is the role of religion (and the veil) in this process of emergence of women out of patriarchal control and towards gender equality?

References

Ma'an News Agency. (2016, June 23). *Palestinian Authority sets municipal elections for October 8.* https://www.maannews.com/Content.aspx?id=771958

Makoyane, N. (1997). TRC women's hearings, Johannesburg, 29 July 1997.

Masote, S. (1997). TRC women's hearings, Johannesburg, 28 July 1997.

McKernan, B. (2016, September 12). Women in Palestine are using Twitter and Facebook to fight back against censorship of their names. *Independent.* http://www.independent.co.uk/news/world/middle-east/women-palestine-fighting-back-censorship-of-names-local-elections-a7238481.html

MEMO. (2016, August 31). Identities of female Palestinian electoral candidates hidden. *Middle East Monitor.* https://www.middleeastmonitor.com/20160831-identities-of-female-palestinian-electoral-candidates-hidden/

Mtintso, T. (1997). Opening speech by Thenjiwe Mtintso, TRC women's hearings, Johannesburg, 28 July 1997, included in the transcript of Sheila Masote's testimony.

Oboe, A. (2007). The TRC women's hearings as performance and protest in the New South Africa. *Research in African Literatures, 38*(3), 60-76. https://muse.jhu.edu/article/221272/pdf

7 Women's role in the Syrian Revolution… Still hope!

Joumana Seif[1]

Is it possible to separate women's rights from human rights in general and is it possible to obtain these rights under a dictatorship regime?

These questions had been raised among activists many years before the outbreak of the Syrian revolution due to the increasing calls to amend the personal status law. They were raised during private and confidential forums. Those who raised them did not have a voice: they were deprived from accessing any platform in light of the prevailing political muteness and emergency law that had been applicable for more than four decades in Syria, and confiscated of all rights and freedom.

Most of the Syrian women activists and political opponents did not get involved in this battle at that time due to their belief that women's rights cannot be separated or disentangled, and due to their belief that it would be meaningless to have delusive gains under a rule that violates all the rights and does not acknowledge citizenship.

When the Syrian revolution began in 2011, Syrian women realized that it was the right moment to demand all rights: freedom, justice and full equality under a civic and democratic state; a state of citizenship and a state that is ruled by the law.

I do not think it is an exaggeration to say that Syrian women had the main role in the outbreak of the revolution, particularly in Damascus. While waiting for the verdict hearing of the activist Ali Al-Abdallah, more than 50 male and

1. Head of the Legal Committee in the Syrian Women's Network, Ghaziantep, Turkey; seifjoumana@gmail.com

How to cite this chapter: Seif, J. (2018). Women's role in the Syrian Revolution… Still hope! In C. Padovani & F. Helm (Eds), *Rethinking the transition process in Syria: constitution, participation and gender equality* (pp. 95-99). Research-publishing.net. https://doi.org/10.14705/rpnet.2018.21.761

female activists, lawyers, and politicians gathered in the hall of the military court. Al-Abdallah had been arrested for writing an article criticizing the politics of Iran and he was sentenced to one year in prison. While waiting, there had been arrangements for a sit-in in front of the ministry of the interior to protest against the conditions of the political prisoners, who announced an open-ended hunger strike inside Adra prison. While male politicians suggested that the sit-in should be restricted to only prisoners' families and wanted to submit a petition including their demands to the minister of the interior; the women insisted on mobilizing and expanding the participation and insisted on raising the ceiling of the demands. The women's views won in the end; there was a mobilization, most of the sitters-in were women, many of them were arrested on that day, and some of them were not released until after a long hunger strike.

These Syrian women leaders, including Razan Zaitouna, believed in democracy and human values and challenged the Syrian regime for many years, as well as the Islamists that kidnapped Zaitouna to silence her voice and the values she believed in.

A few months after the revolution and with the excessive violence of the regime, women felt the danger of approaching violence. They also realized that this would limit women's participation disproportionately given the magnitude of women's presence and their active role. They launched initiatives through which they proved their political stance, which was to support the revolution and peaceful protest and to refuse all forms of violence against protesters, including killing, arresting, and torturing. They also demanded that the revolution be kept peaceful, for this was seen as the unwavering way to bring about the change they aspired to and wanted about the dangerous ramifications of armed actions.

During that time, women worked very hard to mobilize and organize themselves in groups with clear objectives, and they started to further expand their activities and networks in order to include women from other regions, particularly in conservative communities. With the intensification of the regime's repression, women began to work in relief and to provide medications and medical supplies. With the intensification of violence and the arming of the revolution, women were excluded from the fieldwork and many female activists had to flee Syria since they were directly and regularly targeted.

Syrian women did not abandon their responsibilities and their active role even after they left Syria. They started to establish women's organizations, feminist networks, and lobbies to mobilize their efforts and to work on women's issues, needs, and empowerment in all fields and to have their voice heard to obtain decision-making positions and activate their role in the political transition process and envision the future of a democratic Syria.

Syrian Women's Network (SWN) is a non-profit and independent network that was established in May 2013 by a number of organizations and independent individuals. SWN works on active women's participation and civic, political, cultural, and economic empowerment. It also works on raising community awareness to give voice and presence to Syrian women in all international forums. SWN is one of several bodies that have been established. Another example is the Syrian Feminist Lobby that was established in July 2014 to press for an active role and equal participation of women throughout political decision-making processes inside the opposition spectrums that believe in democracy. Additionally, groups of specialized organizations have been established in all fields such as law, constitution, and its engendering.

Since those organizations and networks believed in the peace process and building a new Syria, the Syrian Women's Initiative for Peace and Democracy (SWIPD) was established under the auspices of United Nations (UN) Women. SWIPD distinguishes itself by its inclusiveness for diverse women who have different ideological and political views, yet who could come to a consensus on a group of common principles that bring them together and regulate their work and activities. The Initiative had a lobbying campaign that targeted the UN special envoy to Syria and Ambassadors of pertinent countries to include representatives from the Syrian feminist movement during the negotiations process. SWIPD also participated in the round of negotiations that was held by the Special Envoy (May 2015) during the preparations for launching Geneva III.

Syrian feminist movements, in general, have so far achieved the following:

- the Syrian Women's Advisory Board that works directly with the Special Envoy, Mr De Mistura (despite the many observations on his performance);

- a women's Consultative Group of the High Negotiations Committee;

- three women out of fifteen members in the High Negotiations Committee (the Opposition);

- 30% representation of women in the deliberations of the Civil Society Support Room in the negotiations in Geneva;

- a large number of Syrian women who are politically empowered and prepared to be in decision-making positions.

On a personal note:

I am not satisfied with what we have reached so far and believe that some uncalculated moves have had negative impacts on long years of feminist struggle.

Today, the situation on the ground is appalling, the Russian military intervention and the targeting of schools, hospitals, and civilians in general undermine the efforts for peace, the negotiation process, and political transition. However, we are condemned to hope, we have to continue our efforts to achieve just peace and return to building a new Syria, and I believe that Syrian women have learned a lot from the hard conditions we have experienced and this suffering will impose a new reality on Syrian women, and new relations if we take what it has to offer.

On the civil society level:

In my opinion, if certain conditions are met, the role of women will be totally different after the war and reality will impose the emergence of new women leaders and new relations in a society that is more open and balanced. Women will not accept exclusion or discrimination, especially since the main responsibility for reconstruction will be theirs due to a lack of men, like what happened in Germany after the Second World War. But as I mentioned this cannot be achieved without providing certain conditions.

A fair political solution is needed, based on the Geneva I communiqué, and that would lead to a democratic state and end all forms of tyranny; accompanied by a dignified return of refugees, who should not be forced to return. The transitional justice process should be initiated, because there is no peace without justice. Also, real support should be provided by the West and the friends of Syria, with a comprehensive plan like the Marshall plan, which observes the following:

- reconstruction of the economy to provide job opportunities in all areas of Syria to encourage those involved in fighting to leave their weapons and join the process of rebuilding;

- constructing a new educational system that includes human rights values and a culture of peace;

- strengthening the role of civil society;

- and providing projects aimed at women's economic empowerment.

And the most important and urgent condition for now is that the violence should be stopped and humanitarian aid must be completely separated from the trading of political negotiations and allowed to reach those in need. Water, food, and medicine should not be weapons of war. The siege should be broken. That can help a lot in reducing the suffering and emigration.

8 Rethinking transition in Syria, gender equality, and constitution

Mariam Jalabi[1]

There would be no Syrian revolution without the brave and defiant Syrian women who founded it. Women activists, women human rights leaders, women lawyers, mothers, daughters, sisters; Syrian women have been at the forefront of the Syrian revolution since day one, and they have continued to lead their communities throughout the ensuing bloodshed.

Gender equality remains at the heart of the Syrian revolution as it approaches its sixth year. Without it, the revolution will not achieve its ultimate goals of freedom, dignity, justice, and democracy for Syria's future. However, to achieve gender equality in a future Syria, we must coordinate at every level of decision-making and establish a constitution that institutionalizes a political space in which the equal rights and responsibilities of all Syrian men and women are protected and respected.

Until there is a legal space created to protect women's rights, Syrian women's voices will not be accounted for. The voices of Syrian women who work tirelessly, having maintained an essential role in the revolution since before it began, will go unheard. Women's ability to influence political decisions will be minimal – if not non-existent.

Over the past several years and months, we have seen the international community renew its focus on involving Syrian women in the political process. Too often, our role has been reduced to tokens espousing apolitical positions in favor of peace, but devoid of any stake in this conflict. The reality is that Syrian

1. Syrian Women's Network, Cairo, Egypt; mariam.jalabi@gmail.com

How to cite this chapter: Jalabi, M. (2018). Rethinking transition in Syria, gender equality, and constitution. In C. Padovani & F. Helm (Eds), *Rethinking the transition process in Syria: constitution, participation and gender equality* (pp. 101-105). Research-publishing.net. https://doi.org/10.14705/rpnet.2018.21.762

women are inherently political. We were at the forefront of the revolution and our goals remain those of the revolution: we want a free, democratic Syria, free of Assad's tyranny and the Islamic State of Iraq and Syria's (ISIS) terror. And we will not rest until this is the Syria we have achieved.

While various diplomatic bodies debate Syrian policy, it is vital that the debate provides a clear space for women in Syria's future, including the brave Syrian women who have played a vital role in the Syrian opposition from day one. These women should not be muted. Our political aspirations should not be reduced to sound bites that deny our opposition to a dictator that has killed half a million of our people, gassed our children, and besieged our cities.

Equal inclusion of women in the future of Syria's constitution is critical to achieving a true democratic, pluralistic, and civic state. In a future Syria, equality can only be achieved by institutionalizing a political space for women, enshrining gender parity in the foundation of any political solution to the conflict, and throughout the process of rebuilding. With a gendered constitution in place, Syrian women will have a concrete mechanism they can use to protect their rights.

From the beginning of the revolution, women actively participated in peaceful protests and civil organizing. Subject to less surveillance and scrutiny, women were able to subversively circulate flyers and information. Once the revolution became complicated by the regime's brutal indiscriminate violence against civilians, the revolution was co-opted by men and effectively became a man's domain. Somewhere along the way, women lost the role they had during peaceful uprising, which put them side by side with the men. Despite this, women found ways to continue their work and find their space within a war zone dominated by men. Syrian women are often successful within the realm of negotiations within Syria, having successfully brokered ceasefires, organized deliveries of supplies, and established safe spaces for women and children. Women are often at the forefront of efforts to continue children's education, particularly when they cannot attend school. They are crucial to organizing nonviolent protests, documenting human rights violations, and are often the foundation of civil society. At every level of the Syrian conflict, women play a distinct and constructive role.

Despite this, women are blocked from positions of power in decision-making processes within the Syrian opposition, which remains dominated by men. Although progress has been made to raise awareness and to advocate for greater female participation, without an institutionalized mechanism for political inclusion, we have seen little progress. Women are active in all aspects of the revolution and in fact, broader Syrian society as a whole, yet they are still far from enjoying equal representation and participation in politics, both internally and within the Syrian opposition. Women constitute five percent or less in all recognized Syrian opposition groups, regardless of papers produced stating otherwise. When attempts are made to remedy the lack of women, they are often flawed and do not lead to actual results. Syrian women deserve a say in crafting the decisions that affect them.

On the other hand, the internationally sponsored Syrian political peace processes lack meaningful inclusion of women. The United Nations Special Envoy established a 'Women's Advisory Board' which seems to be its solution for not including women at a decision making level. This does not help women get to a decision making position. On the contrary, it camouflages the issue by suggesting women's presence when in fact they do not have a meaningful seat at the table. The Syrian opposition has responded by creating the 'Women's Consultative Committee'. In both instances the meaningful participation of women in the negotiations will not take place unless women are sitting at the table with men making decisions for the future of the country together. Women's presence at the margins only perpetuates their marginalized status.

Without their inclusion and the guarantee for women's rights, which are human rights, the revolution cannot achieve its goals. There are a number of ways to do so. Creative campaigns to amplify the voices of women who work tirelessly to raise awareness are vital to ensuring that the message is delivered. Syrian women's organizations have organized themselves to lobby political efforts, including a push for a quota and enforcing existing quotas for women's political participation in the Syrian opposition political bodies. However, more must change in order for this shift to fully take place.

One way to achieve this shift is by demonstrating the value of women's political participation. One of the many values in increasing the presence of women is that it diversifies the dialog around a political solution, providing an influx of nuanced outlooks and skills. Women are a huge, relatively untapped resource for information from on the ground in Syria, which would enrich any decision-making or policy. Women are able to effectively connect with others across ethnic and religious lines, enhancing their ability to provide a variety of outlooks on issues.

This ongoing movement for greater political participation espouses equal opportunities for men and women in employment, education, and decision-making. It also advocates for equality in gender roles and personal statuses in the eyes of the state. The goal is to enhance the national unity of Syria and to undertake concrete efforts to ensure legal, constitutional, and social equality for all Syrians, regardless of gender. Enhancing the role of women ensures equality and protects the national unity, which is essential for Syria's future.

This must be approached at three levels: internationally, locally, and socially. At the international level, women must be made responsible for proposing and implementing political solutions. This includes an increase of women's membership in negotiating bodies, political committees, and civil society leadership positions. At a local level, it is essential to work with all elements within Syria to conceptualize and implement action plans for ending the violence. Women must continue to be integrated in local councils, ceasefires, and civil society groups. Lastly, at a social level, the idea of women as leaders must be normalized across spectrums, both on the ground in Syria and in the negotiating rooms of Geneva. To normalize the position of women as leaders is to increase their physical presence in politics and have the agency for their own fate, which is a vital aspect of achieving gender parity in the future.

Finally, I cannot stress enough how difficult it is to make my fellow Syrians prioritize issues like a constitution and gender equality, while our people are being decimated with total impunity. Across Syria, women and men are being starved, tortured, and bombed to death at record rates while the world watches and people like myself discuss the virtues of ending a patriarchal system. Syrian women are being annihilated – tens of thousands have been killed. It is difficult for Syrian women to comprehend that we here in the West can talk seriously about their rights, when we won't take basic steps to protect their lives. Syrian women want and need civilian protection. They are dying without it, and everyday that the world fails to take the action needed to protect Syrian women and men, extremists grow stronger – which as we all know, will hurt Syrian women in the long run. If the world truly wants a free Syria, in which women's rights are protected, then it must stand prepared to protect Syrian civilians by taking the steps to stop the number one killer in Syria: indiscriminate aerial bombardment.

Section 3.

Launching the ABC
for a gender sensitive constitution

This section hosts reflections stemming from a challenging document: the *ABC Gender Sensitive Constitution, a handbook for engendering constitution making*, that has been promoted by IFE-EFI and written by Silvia Suteu (University College of London) and Ibrahim Draji (University of Damascus)[1]. The rationale for elaborating such an 'ABC guide', the challenges in adopting a gender perspective in constitution building, and the wager of moving from normative aspirations to implementation and actual respect of fundamental rights are elaborated upon from academic, advocacy, and political perspectives.

---

1. http://www.efi-ife.org/sites/default/files/ABC%20for%20a%20Gender%20Sensitive%20Constitution.pdf

9 The necessity of engendering the constitution and its content[1]

Ibrahim Draji[2]

"Women are born free, and they enjoy the rights of equality with men in all aspects".

This is Article 1 of the Declaration of the Rights of Woman and Citizenship, which was written by the French women's rights activist Olympe de Gouges in 1791, and was one of the reasons for driving her to the guillotine, where she was killed. The struggle for gender equality had started long before Olympe de Gouges's Declaration, and continued after it. It knew milestones and witnessed many successes and achievements, as well as many failures and frustrations until women attained what they have obtained so far.

During this conference, I presented a guide to a gender sensitive constitution. Gender (Suteu & Draji, 2015) is a very important subject that needs to be tackled through formulating constitutions compatible with a gender perspective, and the existence of a legal obligation to formulate these types of constitutions first. Second, by checking the content of these constitutions and what they should incorporate.

1. First, why are states legally obliged to engender their constitutions?

Today, many people, women and men, support gender equality from different viewpoints: some believe in and adopt gender equality as a human right of

---

1. This presentation has been made via Skype and part of the present article has already been published by the author in Suteu and Draji (2015), reproduced with kind permissions from the copyright holder Euromed Feminist Initiative IFE-EFI.

2. University of Damascus, Damascus, Syria; daraji@unhcr.org

How to cite this chapter: Draji, I. (2018). The necessity of engendering the constitution and its content. In C. Padovani & F. Helm (Eds), *Rethinking the transition process in Syria: constitution, participation and gender equality* (pp. 109-141). Research-publishing.net. https://doi.org/10.14705/rpnet.2018.21.763

---

all genders, others for ethical and religious reasons, others for ideological and political reasons, or for intellectual and philosophical reasons. Some see gender equality as a manifestation of the advancement of civilization. However, regardless of these different starting points, it is necessary to also investigate the legal obligation incumbent upon states to engender their constitutions. To what extent are states legally obliged to respect the principles of equality and non-discrimination between women and men? And what are the major international and regional conventions that deal with engendering the constitution? How important are these treaties in the legal systems of states?

1.1. International instruments[3] mandating gender equality, non-discrimination and engendering the constitution

International law enshrines gender equality as a right and a principle of human rights. The many international documents relevant to gender equality and non-discrimination reflect the attention paid to this issue, on the one hand, and the extent to which this right is violated, on the other.

I outline here, in brief, the major international and regional instruments (conventions, declarations, and resolutions) which address the issues of gender equality, non-discrimination on the basis of gender, and engendering the constitution.

1.1.1. United Nations Charter (1945)[4]

Although the Charter was primarily concerned with the legalization of the international order and the creation of a new international organization to lead the world towards peace after World War II, it did not neglect gender equality

---

3. Some constitutions emphasized that texts relating to rights and freedoms must be interpreted in accordance with international human rights conventions. For example, the Spanish Constitution Article 10, Paragraph 2: "The laws relating to fundamental rights and freedoms recognized by the Constitution shall be interpreted in accordance with the Universal Declaration of Human Rights and the international treaties and conventions ratified by Spain in this regard". As well as the Constitution of Portugal, Article 16, Paragraph 2: "The provisions of this Constitution and the laws relating to fundamental rights shall be interpreted in accordance with the Universal Declaration of Human Rights". Such provisions reinforce the ability of judges to interpret the constitution in accordance with international standards and rely on them in their judgments.

4. https://treaties.un.org/doc/publication/ctc/uncharter.pdf

---

and women's equal enjoyment of all rights, without discrimination. These rights have been tackled in three different places of the Charter. Firstly, in the Preamble, which states: "We, the peoples of the United Nations [...] reaffirm faith in fundamental human rights, in the dignity and worth of the human person, in the equal rights of men and women"; secondly, in Chapter I on the *Purposes and Principles* of the United Nations, where Article 1(3) states: "promoting and encouraging respect for human rights and for fundamental freedoms for all without distinction as to [...] sex"; thirdly, in Chapter IX on *International Economic and Social Cooperation*, where Article 55(c) reaffirms that the United Nations works towards "universal respect for, and observance of, human rights and fundamental freedoms for all without distinction as to [...] sex".

1.1.2. Universal Declaration of Human Rights (1948)[5]

The Universal Declaration of Human Rights reaffirms the right to equality for 'all human beings'. Article 1 states that: "All human beings are born free and equal in dignity and rights. They are endowed with reason and conscience and should act towards one another in a spirit of brotherhood"[6]. It also clearly emphasizes the commitment to prohibiting discrimination in Article 2, which states that: "Everyone is entitled to all the rights and freedoms set forth in this Declaration, without distinction of any kind, such as [...] sex [...] or other status".

1.1.3. International Covenant on Economic, Social, and Cultural Rights (1966)[7]

The Covenant reaffirms the right to equality between women and men. Article 3 states that: "The States Parties to the present Covenant undertake to ensure the equal right of men and women to the enjoyment of all economic, social, and cultural rights set forth in the present Covenant". As for non-discrimination, Article 2(2) of the Covenant states that: "The States Parties to the present Covenant undertake

---

5. http://www.un.org/en/udhrbook/pdf/udhr_booklet_en_web.pdf

6. The Universal Declaration of Human Rights refers to 'brotherhood' which is a reflection of the period in which the document was drafted, and of the lack of awareness of its framers of the contents of this term.

7. http://www.pwescr.org/PWESCR_Handbook_on_ESCR.pdf

to guarantee that the rights enunciated in the present Covenant will be exercised without discrimination of any kind as to […] sex […] or other status".

In Article 2(1), the Covenant refers to the obligation to engender both the constitution and national legislation. This article obliges states to adopt the necessary 'legislative measures' to guarantee the enjoyment of the rights enunciated in the Covenant. It states: "Each State Party to the present Covenant undertakes to take steps, individually and through international assistance and cooperation, especially economic and technical, to the maximum of its available resources, with a view to achieving progressively the full realization of the rights recognized in the present Covenant by all appropriate means, including particularly the adoption of legislative measures". It is noticeable here that the Covenant, after talking about the obligation of states to take 'all means' to realize these rights, focuses particularly on 'legislative measures'. This reflects the priority given to these measures in implementing the rights and principles of the Covenant. Legislation, in its general understanding, here includes any law enacted and issued by the State, including the constitution as the state's supreme law.

1.1.4. International Covenant on Civil and Political Rights (1966)[8]

The Covenant states the right to equality in Article 3 and reaffirms non-discrimination by virtue of Article 2(1). The covenant emphasizes the need to adopt the necessary legislation in order to guarantee that everyone enjoys the rights stipulated, which is stated in Article 2(2).

1.1.5. Convention on the Elimination of all Forms of Discrimination Against Women (CEDAW) (1979)[9]

This Convention is deemed an international bill of women's rights; it defines decisively the actions considered as discriminatory against women and the

---

8. https://treaties.un.org/doc/publication/unts/volume%20999/volume-999-i-14668-english.pdf

9. http://www.ohchr.org/Documents/ProfessionalInterest/cedaw.pdf

---

measures to be taken to eliminate that discrimination. CEDAW reaffirms the principle of equality between women and men throughout its provisions. For example, Article 3 states, as does Article 15(1), that: "States Parties shall take in all fields [...] all appropriate measures [...] to ensure the full development and advancement of women, for the purpose of guaranteeing them the exercise and enjoyment of human rights and fundamental freedoms on a basis of equality with men".

As for non-discrimination, CEDAW has not only used the general language on 'non-discrimination' included in all other conventions. It instead went further and defined the concept of prohibited discrimination and set forth positive steps, such as temporary measures to remove previous discrimination, which has become entrenched through decades of discriminatory practices. CEDAW prohibits discrimination by virtue of Article 2, which states that: "States Parties condemn discrimination against women in all its forms".

CEDAW imposes many obligations on states to incorporate women's rights, gender equality, and the prohibition of discrimination between women and men in their national constitutions and legislation. It also imposes an obligation for states to amend their national legislation and penal provisions that contradict these rights and principles. This is clearly stated in Article 2(a), (b), (c), (f), (j), and (g).

It is noticeable that the Convention, in Article 5(a), asks states to take all appropriate measures to modify the social and cultural patterns of conduct of women and men, with a view of achieving the elimination of prejudices and customary and all other practices which are based on the idea of the inferiority or the superiority of either of the sexes.

1.1.6. United Nations Security Council Resolution 1325 (2000)[10]

The CEDAW Committee has mentioned that "women often take on leadership roles during conflict as heads of households, peacemakers, political leaders, and

---

10. On women and peace and security: http://www.un-documents.net/sr1325.htm

combatants" (CEDAW, 2013, para 6); the Committee has repeatedly expressed concern that their voices are silenced and marginalized in post-conflict and transition periods and recovery processes.

In order to overcome this reality, in 2000, the Security Council adopted Resolution 1325. It reaffirmed the important role of women in the prevention and resolution of conflicts and in peace-building, as well as the need for their equal participation and more prominent role in decision making with regard to conflict prevention and resolution. Moreover, the Security Council has adopted several follow-up resolutions – 1820 (2008), 1888 (2009), 1889 (2009), 1960 (2010), 2106 (2013), and 2122 (2013) – recognizing further aspects of the link between women and peace and security: the use of sexual violence as a tactic of war; its status as a war crime; the obligation of parties to armed conflict to take measures to prevent it; the duty of peacekeeping missions to protect women and children from sexual violence during armed conflict; and setting up a roadmap for the implementation of member states' commitments in this area.

The importance of this resolution lies in the fact that it promotes equality of opportunity for women and men in a field that has never been addressed before by any international or regional convention: conflict resolution and peace processes; women's presence as special representatives and envoys to pursue good offices, incorporating a gender perspective into peacekeeping operations, and the involvement of women in the making and implementation mechanisms of the peace agreements. While novel, there is also synergy between Resolution 1325 and CEDAW, and the United Nations has explained the complementarity between the goals they pursue and the standards they set for the states. Both documents have a gender equality agenda and demand women's full participation at all levels of decision making, both call for legal equality between women and men, and both seek to ensure that women's experiences, needs, and perspectives are incorporated into political, legal, and social decisions.

Resolution 1325 explicitly mentions states' obligations to engender their constitutions. This is stated in Clause 8(c), which reaffirms the state parties' commitment to take "measures that ensure the protection of and respect for human rights of women and girls, particularly as they relate to the constitution, the electoral system, the police, and the judiciary".

1.2.   Regional instruments that mandate gender equality, non-discrimination, and engendering the constitution

There are also regional instruments which set forth obligations for states to recognize the principle of gender equality, prohibit discrimination, and require the engendering of national constitutions.

1.2.1.   European instruments

The European human rights system is one of the most developed regional systems mainly due to the active role of the European Court of Human Rights (ECHR)[11] in sanctioning violations by member states.

The ECHR reaffirms the equality of individuals in the enjoyment of all rights implied in the phrase 'everyone' in its Article 1, which states that: "The High Contracting Parties shall secure to everyone within their jurisdiction the rights and freedoms defined in Section I of this Convention".

Also, the ECHR prohibits discrimination by virtue of Article 14, which states that: "The enjoyment of the rights and freedoms set forth in this Convention shall be secured without discrimination on any ground such as sex [...] or other status". The jurisdictional reach of the ECHR is not limited to the people enjoying the nationality of one of the state parties. Rather, it covers everyone falling under the legal jurisdiction of any of the state parties, such as their residents. Thus, anyone who is under the jurisdiction of a state party enjoys the protection of the convention. This enforcement is the task of the ECHR, which receives complaints from individuals, groups of individuals, and state parties. The court has developed a rich jurisprudence on gender equality and non-discrimination (see Radacic, 2008).

---

11. https://www.coe.int/en/web/conventions/full-list/-/conventions/rms/0900001680063765

In order to ensure more protection and equality and to adopt a general principle prohibiting discrimination in the exercise of all rights included in the law, without specifying one right and neglecting another, Protocol No. 12 to the Convention for the Protection of Human Rights and Fundamental Freedoms was concluded. It was introduced for signing on the 11th of April 2000, and entered into effect in 2005. The Protocol contains a general prohibition of discrimination in Article 1.

The importance of this protocol lies in the fact that it enhances the protection against discrimination afforded by the ECHR and reflects advancements in international legal protection against discrimination. Article 14 of the ECHR, contrary to other international conventions, does not include a separate prohibition of discrimination. Thus, discrimination is prohibited only with regards to "the enjoyment of the rights and freedoms" set forth in the Convention in Article 14. However, when the Protocol came into effect, the prohibition of discrimination acquired 'independent life', separate from other provisions of the ECHR[12].

Gender equality is a fundamental principle of the European Union and is listed, for example, in Article 8 of the Treaty on the Functioning of the European Union (TFEU), which states that: "In all its activities, the Union shall aim to eliminate inequalities, and to promote equality, between men and women" (see European Commission, 2011).

The right to equality is referred to in two places of the Charter of Fundamental Rights of the European Union[13]. The first is in Article 20, which mentions equality before the law in a brief and general way: "Everyone is equal before the law". The second is in Article 23, which explicitly enunciates gender equality, as well as the possibility of adopting affirmative action measures[14].

---

12. For more details on this protocol, see the Council of Europe website: http://www.coe.int/ar_JO/web/compass/legal-protection-of-human-rights

13. http://www.europarl.europa.eu/charter/pdf/text_en.pdf

14. See further Handbook on European non-discrimination law March. (2011). http://fra.europa.eu/en/publication/2011/handbook-european-non-discrimination-law

1.2.2. African instruments

The African Charter on Human and Peoples' Rights[15] has been the starting point for a new era in the area of human rights in Africa. It reaffirms the right to absolute equality in Article 3. As for the principle of non-discrimination, it is reaffirmed in Article 2 of the Charter, which states that: "Every individual shall be entitled to the enjoyment of the rights and freedoms recognized and guaranteed in the present Charter without distinction of any kind such as [...] sex [...] or any other status".

The Protocol on Women's Rights[16] in Africa reaffirms the principle of legal equality between women and men. Article 8 of the Protocol states that: "Women and men are equal before the law and shall have the right to equal protection and benefit of the law". As for the principle of non-discrimination, Article 2(1) of the Protocol states that: "State Parties shall combat all forms of discrimination against women".

This obligation is reaffirmed in the Protocol on the Rights of Women in Africa. It states explicitly the obligation of states to include the principles of non-discrimination and gender equality in their constitutions and legislation. It also allows for affirmative action measures to redress continuing discrimination against women.

1.2.3. American instruments

We refer here to the American Declaration of the Rights and Duties of Man (1948) that affirms equality and non-discrimination in its Article 2. The American Convention on Human Rights (1969)[17] declares the duty of state parties as protecting the rights of all persons under their jurisdiction, without

---

15. http://www.humanrights.se/wp-content/uploads/2012/01/African-Charter-on-Human-and-Peoples-Rights.pdf

16. http://www.achpr.org/files/instruments/women-protocol/achpr_instr_proto_women_eng.pdf

17. http://www.oas.org/dil/treaties_B-32_American_Convention_on_Human_Rights.pdf

discrimination on the basis of, among other grounds, 'sex'[18], and the right to equal protection of the laws for all, "without discrimination" (Article 24).

In a separate article on the rights of the family, the convention affirms the principle of non-discrimination with regard to marriage (Article 17(2)) and also calls upon states to "take appropriate steps to ensure the equality of rights and the adequate balancing of responsibilities of the spouses as to marriage, during marriage, and in the event of its dissolution" (Article 17(4)). The Inter-American Court of Human Rights adjudicates on disputes involving state parties accused of having violated their obligations under the convention and has developed a rich jurisprudence on gender equality and non-discrimination (Palacios Zuolaga, 2008). The Inter-American Commission on Human Rights has also collated the legal standards applicable to gender equality in the InterAmerican system emerging from the court's jurisprudence and state practice (IACHR, 2015).

1.2.4. Arab instruments

States of the Arab region suffer from lack of regional sources concerning human rights in general and women's rights in particular. This is in spite of the pressing need for such instruments, owing to the restrictions imposed on Arab women in many countries, either because of harsh discriminative constitutional and legislative provisions, or because of religious concepts and social customs. The main regional instrument is the Arab Charter on Human Rights (2004)[19] which was adopted by the 16th Arab Summit hosted by Tunisia on the 23rd of May 2004.

The Charter reaffirms the principle of equality in more than one clause and in more than one form. Article 3(2) suggests undertaking "necessary measures to guarantee effective equality in the enjoyment of all rights and [freedoms] established in the present Charter, so as to protect against all forms of

---

18. This article and the previous one refer to 'sex' rather than 'gender'. This should be read in the light of the date of these instruments, in 1948 and 1968, respectively, early in the history of international attention to issues of gender equality and non-discrimination.

19. http://www.eods.eu/library/LAS_Arab%20Charter%20on%20Human%20Rights_2004_EN.pdf

discrimination". Article 11 states that: "All persons are equal before the law and have the right to enjoy its protection without discrimination". Article 12 also reaffirms that: "All persons are equal before the courts and tribunals"[20].

The Charter also refers to non-discrimination and affirmative action in two separate paragraphs of Article 3. Article 3(1) declares "the right to enjoy all the rights and freedoms recognized herein, without any distinction on grounds of [...] sex", and Article 3(3) states: "Men and women are equal in respect of human dignity, in rights and in duties within the framework of the positive discrimination established in favor of women by Islamic Shari'a and other divine laws, legislation and international instruments".

However, by conditioning gender equality and women's rights to the religious framework, the Charter appears to allow for discrimination against women. This is manifested in the fact that 'positive discrimination' is attributed to religious laws, and then to the applicable legislation and instruments, which leaves open the possibility to deny women some of their rights. Therefore, the use of affirmative action in this context – linking it to divine laws – would have the same results as reservations raised with regard to international human rights conventions: both undermine women's rights and justify discrimination against them. This "positive discrimination established in favor of women by [...] divine laws", in Article 3(3), differs radically from the original meaning of affirmative action and the purposes for which it has been developed. Eventually, it can be said that, among all international and regional charters and conventions, the Arab Charter provides the least protection of women's rights and gender equality as per international law standards.

This issue is addressed in Article 44 of the charter, which states that: "The States Parties undertake to adopt, in accordance with their constitutional processes and with the provisions of the present Charter, [whatever legislative or non-legislative] measures in order to give effect on the rights recognized by the present Charter".

---

20. https://www.unicef.org/tdad/arabcharterhumanrights.doc

The main weakness of this charter is that it states that all rights and obligations placed on states shall be in accordance with the constitution or legislation in effect. Thus, states shall take the necessary measures to fulfill the rights set forth in the charter "in accordance with their constitutional processes" according to the aforementioned Article 44.

For example, the measures that enable a child to acquire her/his mother's nationality must be "in accordance with their domestic laws" (Article 29(2)[21]). Another example is the enjoyment of the freedom of thought, conscience and religion, which is limited by the constraints set forth in the law in effect (Article 30(1)).

The risk associated with such references to the constitution and domestic laws in effect stems from the fact that national law may contain many shortcomings. National laws may themselves violate the simplest principles of equality and establish systematically discriminatory practices. Thus, taking this national legislation as the reference to granting rights could only mean further denial of rights and could protect discriminatory practices instead of abolishing them.

Based on the aforementioned, it becomes clear that the obligation to engender the constitution is a binding international legal obligation, with clear legal sources. Women's rights-related international conventions are agreements of a universal and regional nature which apply to the majority of the world's states. It must be noted that the continents are unequal in terms of their recognition of these rights, and there is an obvious lack of recognition of equality between women and men in Asia, especially in the Arab region, either through delaying the ratification of international relevant commitments or through making reservations that empty the commitments of meaning.

It is clear to us how international law is binding for the signatory/member States. They have to implement these treaties 'in good faith', and incorporate them into their national legislation, which may not be invoked as an excuse or justification

---

21. https://www.unicef.org/tdad/arabcharterhumanrights.doc

for evading the implementation of the obligations under those treaties. This was clearly stated in the Vienna Convention on the Law of Treaties of 1969[22] under Articles 26 and 27. The obligation to engender their constitutions and all national legislation is binding upon states as a means to attain the end of ensuring gender equality and protection from all forms of discrimination. Chapter 3 of the ABC for Gender Sensitive Constitutions (Suteu & Draji, 2015) details the content of a gender sensitive constitution, looking at both general principles and specific rights which must be adopted in order to ensure full protection of women's rights, gender equality, and non-discrimination. In spite of this, many international and regional conventions, especially those related to women's right or human rights in general, did not leave their implementation and the incorporation of their content in national legislation to the general rules of international law, but have laid down special provisions at the core of the treaties, themselves obliging contracting states to amend their constitutions and other national legislation to ensure compatibility with their obligations to ensure women's rights, including equality and non-discrimination in the exercise of those rights and the enjoyment of the freedoms contained therein. This is the essence of the term 'gender of the constitution', i.e. the incorporation of its provisions to guarantee women the exercise of all their rights without derogation or discrimination and to eliminate any obstacles to this.

2.   Second, what must a democratic gender-sensitive constitution contain?

Here I present the content of a democratic gender sensitive constitution, as drawn from international law and comparative constitutional design.

2.1.   Principles of a democratic gender sensitive constitution

In the simplest understanding, a democratic constitution is one that is democratically ratified and ensures the establishment and maintenance of a

---

22. https://treaties.un.org/doc/publication/unts/volume%201155/volume-1155-i-18232-english.pdf

democratic system. On the 20th of December 2004, the United Nations General Assembly adopted a resolution in which it defined the basic elements of democracy[23].

According to this resolution, a democratic constitution has to guarantee human rights and freedoms, to incorporate a plural political system, ensure transparency and accountability, guarantee the rule of law, the separation of powers, and the independence of the judiciary. Moreover, it must take into account some basic issues concerning the process of constitution making and not only the constitution's content.

A gender sensitive constitution is a constitution that

- adopts a gender perspective and pays attention to how issues of gender are dealt with and how provisions of the constitution impact on gender,

- ensures substantive gender equality, theoretically and practically,

- prohibits discrimination based on gender, ethnicity, class, color, sexual orientation, age, and other characteristics,

- adopts gender sensitive language (more on this in Suteu & Draji, 2015, chapter 4), and

- contains rules and guarantees to activate this equality and empower women to exercise all their rights, including the possibility of having affirmative action measures to counter discriminatory practices against women.

There are basic principles that constitutions have to stand on and also clear criteria that no democratic constitution can ignore, especially if it is intended to be gender sensitive. If the principles of freedom, dignity, equality, and non-

---

23. See http://undocs.org/A/RES/59/201

discrimination are among the fundamental principles that any constitution must contain, there are also others closely relevant to a democratic constitution and of special importance for women's rights and gender equality. The latter provide guarantees that can be relied on in order to ensure women's enjoyment of their full rights and to abolish the discriminatory practices targeting them. We address here the principles of freedom, dignity, equality, non-discrimination, separation of powers, popular sovereignty as the source of constitutional authority, as well as secularism.

2.1.1. Freedom

Freedom has been recognized as a fundamental principle on which the legal organization of states stands, and which must be included in national constitutions[24]. In addition to recognizing a number of rights and freedoms (such as the freedom of thought, religion, and conscience; the freedom of speech and expression; the freedom of assembly; and the freedom of association, etc.), the constitution should stipulate that it guarantees rights as universal and inalienable, indivisible, interdependent, and interrelated. The list of rights included in the constitution should not be exhaustive. In that way, when necessary, the protection of the constitution could be extended to more rights than those listed explicitly in its text. Such an approach reaffirms that the origin of the rights included in the constitution is freedom and that any limitation of freedom must be subject to the controls set forth in the constitution itself. For example: the Venezuelan constitution, Article 2: "Venezuela constitutes itself as a [...] State [...] which holds as superior values of its legal order and actions [...] those of [...] liberty".

2.1.2. Dignity

Human dignity is one of the most important values that must be enunciated in national constitutions for both women and men alike. Therefore, the constitutions

---

24. However, the French Declaration itself was discriminatory against women, and the failure of the French Revolution to promote women's rights prompted Olympique de Gouge to publish the Declaration on the Rights of Women and [Female] Citizen in 1791.

of many countries include this principle in their preambles or in separate provisions. Examples: South African constitution, Article 1: "The Republic of South Africa is one, sovereign, democratic state founded on the following values: 1. Human dignity". German constitution, Article 1(1): "Human dignity shall be inviolable. To respect and protect it shall be the duty of all state authority".

2.1.3. Equality

National constitutions are the "framework for the elimination of discrimination against women. An explicit constitutional guarantee of gender equality is fundamental to combating discrimination against women and girls in law and in practice"[25]. National constitutions adopt the principle of equality in many formulations.

- Some constitutions enunciate it in general statements without specifying that it applies to both women and men like. For example: the Spanish constitution, Section 14: "Spaniards are equal before the law".

- Other constitutions enunciate equality between women and men specifically. Like the Belgian constitution, Article 10: "Equality between women and men is guaranteed".

- Other constitutions not only enunciate explicitly the equality between women and men, but also acknowledge that formal constitutional equality alone is not enough unless associated with affirmative action steps that must be taken by the State in order to activate this right and empower women to overcome decades of inequality and discriminatory practices against them. They oblige the State to ensure this equality and to take the necessary measures to implement it in practice. An example for that is the Canadian Charter of Rights and Freedoms, Article 15 on "Equality Rights": "(1) Every individual is equal before and under the law and has the right to the equal protection and equal benefit of the

---

25. http://ohchr.org/Documents/Issues/Women/WG/Family/A.HRC.29.40_E.pdf

law without discrimination and, in particular, without discrimination based on race, national or ethnic origin, color, religion, sex, age or mental or physical disability. (2) Subsection (1) does not preclude any law, program or activity that has as its object the amelioration of conditions of disadvantaged individuals or groups including those that are disadvantaged because of race, national or ethnic origin, color, religion, sex, age or mental or physical disability".

Contrary to these good practices, there are some constitutions that disregard and ignore this right, or empty it of any meaning and restrict it in a way that prevents women from benefitting from it. Yemeni constitution, Article 31: "Women are the sisters of men. They have rights and duties, which are guaranteed and assigned by Shari'ah and stipulated by law".

Here, the constitution makers avoided using the term 'equality', preferring instead to use 'sisters of men', which does not have a clear meaning and may be interpreted in a restrictive way. Moreover, the text further undermines gender equality by describing the source of women's rights, as sisters of men, as being sharia and national legislation rather than any clearly defined international norm or convention. This allows for interpretations which may empty gender equality of meaning and deny women their rights. The constitution of Yemen, however, is not the only one in this regard. For example: Iranian constitution, Article 20: "All citizens of the country, both men and women, equally enjoy the protection of the law and enjoy all human, political, economic, social, and cultural rights, in conformity with Islamic criteria". Clearly, though this constitution uses the term 'equality' between women and men, it restricts this supposed equality by subjecting it to 'Islamic criteria', which are, in turn, subject to religious men's different interpretations and explanations.

Numerous constitutions have created constitutional bodies tasked with promoting gender equality and removing all forms of discrimination between women and men[26]. They should have a clear mandate to deal with and follow

---

26. For a review of institutions in the OSCE region, see http://www.osce.org/odihr/97756

up on equality issues, and should possess the competence and capacity to enable them to achieve the objective for which they have been established.

The United Nations[27] has adopted a set of minimum standards applicable to national human rights institutions which include women's rights and gender equality bodies. These principles require that the body have a broad and clear mandate, autonomy from the government, independence, pluralist membership, adequate resources, and adequate powers of investigation. For example, the Ecuadorian constitution, Article 156: "The National Equality Councils are bodies responsible for ensuring the full observance and exercise of the rights enshrined in the Constitution and in international human rights instruments. The Councils shall exercise their attributions for the drafting, cross-cutting application, observance, follow-up and evaluation of public policies involving the issues of gender".

It should be highlighted that these bodies are not ends in themselves. Rather, they are means to realize a higher end, which is both formal and substantive equality between women and men. Thus, it is not sufficient to stipulate the creation of these bodies in the constitution and then leave them inactive and powerless, as experience in many countries reveals. Their financial and administrative independence must be set forth in the constitution in order for these bodies not to be manipulated or suppressed by political authorities. They should also not be left vulnerable to budgetary cutbacks, as experience shows that in times of austerity, cuts to public spending disproportionally affect gender equality institutions[28].

It may also be best not to go into detail in the constitution itself about the competences and procedures guiding the operation of these bodies in order for them to have the necessary flexibility to perform their tasks[29]. Such details will be mandated in implementing legislation and are not what will guarantee the proper

---

27. http://www.ohchr.org/EN/ProfessionalInterest/Pages/StatusOfNationalInstitutions.aspx

28. See http://www.womenlobby.org/IMG/pdf/the_price_of_austerity_-_web_edition.pdf

29. See Suteu and Draji (2015, chapter 4).

---

operation of these bodies. This will be guaranteed by the political will behind creating such bodies and enabling them to work under the best circumstances. Otherwise, they will remain mere bureaucratic structures created in response to international pressure, with no political commitment behind them. This has been the case of Morocco, where the creation of such a body was set forth in law, but the institution has not actually been created.

2.1.4. Non-discrimination

Constitutions must explicitly forbid discrimination. This is a basic principle that may not be ignored or disregarded. For example, the constitution of South Africa prohibits all forms of discrimination, whether exercised by the state or individuals. It also obliges the state to make legislation to combat it. For instance: the South African constitution, Article 9(3): "The state may not unfairly discriminate directly or indirectly against anyone on one or more grounds, including race, gender, sex [...]. No person may unfairly discriminate directly or indirectly against anyone [...]. National legislation must be enacted to prevent or prohibit unfair discrimination".

Other constitutions adopt another option by shedding light on the most common practices of discrimination against women and prohibiting them explicitly. They not only prohibit discrimination generally and explicitly, but prohibit certain practices by name as well. This is the case of the Portuguese constitution, which concentrates, in Article 109, on discrimination against women in the field of "access to political office". The constitution of Ecuador guarantees, in Article 43(1), freedom from discrimination to pregnant and breast-feeding women in "education, social, and labor sectors". Additionally, gender sensitive constitutions have to clearly prohibit both direct and indirect discrimination. Sometimes, indirect discrimination can be more serious as it is hidden and not enough attention is paid to it. This happens

> "when laws, public policies and programmes are built on seemingly gender-neutral criteria, [while in practice they] have a detrimental impact on women. [The risk here is that these] laws, policies and

programmes may unintentionally perpetuate the consequences of past discrimination. They may be inadvertently modelled on male lifestyles and thus fail to take into account aspects of women's life experiences which may differ from those of men. These differences may exist because of stereotypical expectations, attitudes and behaviour directed towards women which are based on the biological differences between women and men. They may also exist because of the generally existing subordination of women by men" (footnote 1[30]).

Examples of indirect discrimination include unnecessary requirements in the workplace which place one gender at a disadvantage compared to the other (such as by discriminating against women who have taken maternity leave or are the primary caregivers in their family). Therefore, constitution makers must address both direct and indirect discrimination when drafting the prohibition of gender based discrimination in the constitution. This will enable them to also combat existing hidden discriminatory practices.

2.1.5. Separation of powers

Respect for the separation of powers principle also has positive implications for women's rights and gender equality because it prevents the different branches of power from cooperating to restrict or ignore them. For example, if the legislative power failed to enact laws related to women's rights, or if the executive power insisted on ignoring the application of these rights, the independent judicial power would be the real guarantor to resort to. The principle of the separation of powers is set forth in most constitutions of the states of the world. For example, the Portuguese constitution, Article 2: "The Portuguese Republic shall be a democratic state based on the rule of law [...] and the separation and interdependence of powers".

Some constitutions even include the separation of powers among principles not open to amendment. Example of the Brazilian constitution, Article 60(4): "No

---

30. http://www.un.org/womenwatch/daw/cedaw/recommendations/General%20recommendation%2025%20(English).pdf

proposal of amendment shall be considered which is aimed at abolishing: III –
the separation of the Government Powers".

2.1.6. Popular sovereignty as the source of constitutional authority

Constitutions must address the source of sovereignty, meaning they must
clarify the authority from which the branches of power derive their jurisdictions
and manifestations of power. It is worth mentioning that recognizing popular
sovereignty as the source of constitutional authority is not only a basis of equality
among all citizens, but allows for the removals of the guardianship of clergies,
regardless of their creed, over societal affairs and subsequent discrimination on
the basis of religious belief. The overwhelming majority of constitutional and
political systems throughout the world tend to adopt popular sovereignty as the
basis of constitutional authority. This is a requirement of democracy itself. For
example: the Italian constitution, Article 1: "Sovereignty belongs to the people,
which exercises it in the forms and within the limits of the Constitution".

2.1.7. Secularism

Secularism refers to the separation of religion and religious institutions
from the decision-making processes of the government and the legislature
and judiciary, so that political and legislative institutions are independent of
religious institutions. Thus, religious affairs should be viewed as personal
matters by the State. This issue is very important and has serious repercussions
for women's rights and freedoms. Women also differ in terms of religion and
beliefs, which makes them subject to different, and sometimes contradictory,
legal systems in countries where religious or traditional authorities also
exercise legal and political power.

Many constitutions in the world explicitly affirm the State's secularism, and
enunciate this in different ways. The French constitution, for example, stipulates
the secularism of the French Republic, reaffirming in the same article the 'respect
to all beliefs'. For example: the French constitution, Article 1 of the Preamble:
"France shall be a [...] secular [power]. It shall respect all beliefs".

Other constitutions adopt a clearer way to reinforce that the State must not ascribe to a religion and must not interfere with or oblige anyone to follow any religion. They also affirm the equality among religious associations representing all religions, which must be separate from the state. The example of the Russian constitution, Article 14: "1. The Russian Federation is a secular state. No state or obligatory religion may be established. 2. Religious associations shall be separate from the State and shall be equal before the law".

It is also necessary for a secular constitution to be a democratic one, as each has its own foundations and principles that must be realized. A secular constitution can also be undemocratic – an example of which is the Turkish constitution which adopts secularism clearly but also includes many provisions that violate democratic principles. Supporters of gender equality and non-discrimination should not barter a democratic constitution for a secular one; instead, they should work to ensure that the gender sensitive constitution they seek to bring about is democratic and secular at the same time.

Incorporating these principles into the constitution will significantly serve women's rights and gender equality. Women are still denied their fundamental rights in many countries, either owing to clear discriminative legal texts, or because of religious beliefs and discriminatory social practices. Therefore, the inclusion and protection of these principles in the constitution will have a significant positive impact on women's rights and gender requirements, as it will provide a constitutional basis that can be legally relied on to forbid many unjust practices that target women and deny them their individual rights[31].

2.2. Rights and freedoms in a gender sensitive constitution

Rights and freedoms occupy a high status in most constitutional documents. A constitution is not a mere document describing the form of the state and its system of governance and regulating the relations among the branches of power. It is also a document that guarantees individual rights and freedoms (Kedzia,

---

31. For more on constitutions providing a legal basis for women's empowerment, see Suteu and Draji (2015, chapter 1).

2013, p. 8 and beyond). In addition to the clear protection of individual rights in general, gender sensitive constitutions must contain specific provisions ensuring women's human right to protection against abuse and discrimination. Constitutions must provide women with an enabling environment in which to exercise their rights and overcome the obstacles restraining them.

2.2.1. The content of constitutional rights

A constitutional document must state, in clear, precise, and detailed terms, all of the civil, political, economic, social, and cultural rights it protects, up to what has become to be known as 'the third generation of rights', which include, among others, the right to a safe environment and sustainable development. Among the constitutions that follow this approach is the constitution of Brazil, which contains 78 articles on rights and freedoms. The same is true for the Colombian constitution, which contains 76 articles on rights on freedoms. This is also the case of the constitution of South Africa, which allocates Chapter II completely to rights and freedoms, under the title of "Bill of Rights" and covers the rights in detail. Of course, it is not just the list of rights included in the constitution which is important, but the extent to which they are enforced. Nevertheless, having a comprehensive bill of rights in the constitution can provide the legal basis for women's empowerment and for achieving further protections in the future.

In addition to the drafting of an accurate text containing clear statements of the general individual rights to be included in the constitutional document, there are other measures that must be included in the constitution to strengthen the constitutional rights of women and ensure their actual enjoyment thereof. This includes clearly enunciating women's right to exercise the freedoms that they have traditionally been denied, such as their sexual and reproductive rights, the right to hold political and judicial positions, labor-related rights, rights of inheritance, freedom within marriage, and the freedom to choose a partner. Therefore, certain constitutions, despite their assertion that 'all citizens' enjoy 'all rights', reaffirm in clear terms the equality between women and men in their enjoyment of certain rights.

Many constitutions also contain texts concerning the creation of agencies aiming to ensure the activation of the rights enshrined in the constitutions. These are given different names: Ombudsman, Gender Equality Ombudsman, Human Rights Commission, Human Rights Ombudsman, Human Rights Protection Committee, etc. Regardless of the name, they have to possess real powers and not be merely supervisory or consultative bodies.

2.2.2. Rights to sexual and reproductive health and to bodily integrity and autonomy

A gender sensitive constitution must provide for women's health, including for their sexual and reproductive health. A good starting point is recognizing reproductive rights as human rights as the United Nations has done (HR/PUB/14/6, 2014). As declared in the 1995 Beijing Platform for Action:

> "The human rights of women include their right to have control over and decide freely and responsibly on matters related to their sexuality, including sexual and reproductive health, free of coercion, discrimination and violence. Equal relationships between women and men in matters of sexual relations and reproduction, including full respect for the integrity of the person, require mutual respect, consent and shared responsibility for sexual behavior and its consequences" (Beijing Declaration and Platform for Action, 1995, para 96).

Women's sexual and reproductive health is connected with many human rights, including the right to life, the right not to be exposed to torture, the right to health, the right to privacy, the right to education, and the prohibition of discrimination. This places specific obligations on States, as reaffirmed by the Special Rapporteur on the Right of Everyone to the Enjoyment of the Highest Attainable Standard of Physical and Mental Health, who refers to women's right to access reproductive healthcare services, goods, and facilities that are:

- available in adequate numbers;

- accessible physically and economically;

- accessible without discrimination; and

- of good quality[32].

Violations of women's reproductive rights take numerous forms and include:

"denial of access to services that only women require, or poor quality services, subjecting women's access to services to third party authorization, and performance of procedures related to women's reproductive and sexual health without the woman's consent, including forced sterilization, forced virginity examinations, and forced abortion; [female genital mutilation and early marriage also constitute risks for women's sexual and reproductive rights]"[33].

Acknowledging differences in reproductive biology between women and men is not akin to endorsing paternalism or the view that "biology is destiny" (Irving, 2008, pp. 192-193). Instead, "a gendered perspective on health includes, besides examining differences in health needs, looking at differences between women and men in risk factors and determinants, severity and duration, differences in perceptions of illness, in access to and utilization of health services, and in health outcomes"[34]. The constitutional recognition of the particular needs and vulnerability of women when pregnant, during childbirth, and when caring for their children is a duty incumbent upon the state and is based on the needs associated to that vulnerability, not on the assumption of incapacity (Irving, 2008, pp. 194).

Despite rights to sexual and reproductive health being seldom included in constitutional texts, newer constitutions have begun to recognize their special importance. Like for example the Ecuadorian constitution, Article 32:

---

32. A/61/338

33. Sexual and Reproductive Health and Rights Office of the United Nations High Commissioner for Human Rights. See http://www.ohchr.org/AR/Issues/Women/WRGS/Pages/HealthRights.aspx

34. https://www1.umn.edu/humanrts/edumat/IHRIP/circle/modules/module4.htm

"Health is a right guaranteed by the State [...] by means of economic, social, cultural, educational, and environmental policies; and the permanent, timely and non-exclusive access to programs, actions and services promoting and providing integral healthcare, sexual health, and reproductive health. The provision of healthcare services shall be governed by the principles of equity, universality, solidarity, interculturalism, quality, efficiency, effectiveness, prevention, and bioethics, with a gender and generational approach".

2.2.3. Right to protection from gender based violence

Gender based violence is a major challenge hindering women's ability to exercise many rights and a major violation affecting their rights to life, physical integrity, and human dignity. It occurs all over the world and is used to deny women and girls security, freedom, and the right to life. It is important to take into consideration that not only actual violence constitutes a barrier to freedom, but also the threat of violence. Thus, constitution makers must pay attention to this issue and devote resources to combatting it. Like for example, the Tunisian constitution, Article 46: "The State takes all necessary measures in order to eradicate violence against women".

When formulating the constitutional provisions relevant to the right to protection against gender based violence, this issue should be stated clearly in a separate article and not incorporated into other rights, such as the right to life, physical integrity, or into the provisions of other articles. It will be useful to emphasize it in a clear, accurate, and separate article, as in the case of the Tunisian constitution. Also, the text of the proposed article must clearly state both women's right not to be subjected to this violence, and the state's duty to take all necessary measures to ensure this right and to protect victims of gender based violence[35].

---

35. For clarification on the terminology of "gender based violence", and how it differs from references to "violence against women", see the Glossary included in Suteu and Draji (2015).

2.2.4. Preventing women's rights violations under the pretext of religion or social customs

The violation of women's rights under the pretext of religion, culture or customs/ traditions also hinders women's enjoyment of their human rights. Whereas gender based violence is often prohibited by the constitution or ordinary legislation (even if the latter may be poorly enforced), violating women's rights under the pretext of religion or customs is often justified and legitimized by many who may view it not as a violation but as compliance with religious or customary law. This is often the view taken in countries where sharia is a source of law or the basic or exclusive source of law. This risk is even higher when constitutions explicitly restrict women's rights by stating that they must not contradict religion or custom, or when they make religion and custom, rather than the constitution, the basis for such rights. Therefore, great caution must be exerted when including any reference to existing customs in the constitution. For example, the constitution of South Africa recognizes the roles and rights of religious, cultural, and linguistic communities, but it ensures that their exercise of these rights may not contradict the constitutional bill of rights (Article 31). Then, the same constitution recognizes traditional leaders, allows their legislation to be applied, and mandates that courts apply customary law but only "subject to the Constitution" (Article 211).

The constitution of Venezuela, after recognizing rights of religious communities, restrains the exercise of their beliefs in Article 59, which states that: "no one shall invoke religious beliefs or discipline as a means of evading compliance with law or preventing another person from exercising his or her rights". The essential point that constitution makers have to highlight is that the application of religious and customary law depends on their compatibility with the constitution, especially the constitutional bill of rights, and not the opposite. This has to be projected in explicit and clear statements. This is also the position of the Working Group on the Issue of Discrimination against Women in Law and Practice. In its report of 2015, it recommended that states "recognize and enshrine, in their constitutions and laws, the right to equality, which should apply in all areas of life and have primacy over all religious, customary and indigenous laws, norms, codes and rules, with no possibility of exemption, waiver or circumvention"[36].

This subject is especially important in societies that are still under religious or customary authority. There, the interpreters of religious texts, and not the texts themselves, wield public authority, and their interpretations supersede the constitution. It must be highlighted that all legal texts require an authority to interpret them. The problem is not this openness to interpretation, but who has the power to interpret and give the final say with regard to legal texts: a religious power or a civil one, i.e. a judge. A gender sensitive constitution requires a secular authority interpreting its provisions; otherwise, the protections it offers women risk being undermined in the name of religion[37].

The importance of the above is not limited to the protection of women from the violation of their rights under the pretext of religion or customs. It also ensures that no legislation will be enacted later based on religion or customs, regardless of its contradiction with women's constitutional rights and gender equality. This occurs specifically with regard to regulations on the family, eligibility for public office, inheritance, and personal status laws.

2.2.5. Women's right to participate in public and political life

Constitutions have to ensure all women's political rights, especially the right to popular participation in the administration of public affairs, the right to candidacy and voting in periodic elections through public, equal and secret ballot, and the right to hold public offices and exercise all public functions created pursuant to national legislation, including women's enjoyment of their right to get opportunities to represent their governments at the international level and to take part in the activities of international organizations.

---

36. Report of the Working Group on Discrimination against Women in Law and Practice A/HRC/29/40, Human Rights Council, Twenty-ninth session, 2 April 2015, http://undocs.org/en/A/HRC/29/40

37. For more on an independent judiciary as a necessary guarantee for the constitution's implementation, see Suteu and Draji (2015, chapter 5).

The Beijing Platform of Action adopted at the Fourth International Women's Conference (1995) urged the governments of the world to increase women's participation in decision making positions so as to reach not less than 30% – the goal set by the Economic and Social Council.

The purpose is to reach parity between women and men as a mechanism to realize complete equality. However, international progress on the realization of women's political representation goals, as set by the international community, is still very slow and far from meeting these objectives. Thus, a gender sensitive constitution should stipulate an obligation to address women's exclusion and enable women to hold public office and to participate in elected bodies, including participation in the State's political and public life; the exercise of legislative, judicial, executive, and administrative powers; as well as participation in all aspects of public administration and policy formulation and implementation at international, national, regional, and local levels. This participation must also extend to civil society, including general assemblies and boards, as well as to organizations such as political parties, trade unions, professional or industrial associations, women's organizations, community organizations, and other organizations active in public and political life. However, constitution makers have to take into account that the mere recognition of the equality principle is not sufficient to redress women's exclusion and to enable them to actually participate in the political and public life of the country. That is why the CEDAW Committee has stated that:

> "the principle of equality of women and men has been affirmed in the constitutions and laws of most countries and in all international instruments. Nonetheless, in the last 50 years, women have not achieved equality, and their inequality has been reinforced by their low level of participation in public and political life" (CEDAW, 1997).

Therefore, the Committee affirmed that, while it is necessary to remove impediments in law, this is not sufficient; affirmative action measures must be adopted so as to realize equality of participation[38].

---

38. Committee on the Elimination of Discrimination against Women Sixteenth session (1997) General Recommendation No. 23 United Nations document A / 52/38; http://www.refworld.org/docid/453882a622.html

For example, the Italian constitution affirms the right of citizens of both sexes to hold public office and obliges the State's authorities to adopt specific measures to promote equal opportunities between women and men. The example of the Italian constitution, Article 51: "All citizen of either sex is eligible for public offices and elected positions on equal terms, according to the conditions established by law. To this end, the Republic shall adopt specific measures to promote equal opportunities between women and men".

A broad set of such measures exists, including[39]:

- appointing female candidates,

- modifying the electoral procedures,

- enacting binding laws for political parties to include women on their lists, and

- specifying numeric objectives and quotas in elected bodies, executive bodies and judicial organs. For example, the constitution of Ecuador states explicitly that women must be able to hold judicial offices, including membership of the Constitutional Court on a basis of "parity with men".

The example of the Ecuadorian constitution, Article 434:

"Members [of the Constitutional Court] shall be elected [...] through a public examination process, with citizen oversight and option for challenging the process. In the membership of the Court, efforts shall be made to ensure parity between men and women".

A constitution may also contain a rule stating that no gender may constitute less than a certain percentage of any public body's membership, for example

---

39. To review the use of the quota for women in Europe, see: http://www.europarl.europa.eu/document/activities/cont/200 903/20090310ATT51390/20090310ATT51390EN.pdf.

stating that "neither gender should occupy more than 60% or less that 40% of the positions on a party list or in a decision-making body" (Dahlerup, 2005, p. 142). An example of this is the constitution of Kenya, which states that no more than two-thirds of the members of elective or appointed bodies shall be of the same gender. This ensures that at least one third of a body's members will be of the 'other gender'. The Kenyan constitution makes it obligatory, in Article 27(8), for the state "to take legislative and other measures to implement the principle that not more than two-thirds of the members of elective or appointive bodies shall be of the same gender". This is reaffirmed in Article 81, which states that: "The electoral system shall comply with the following principles— (b) not more than two-thirds of the members of elective public bodies shall be of the same gender".

The purpose of affirmative measures is to achieve parity between women and men on the way to realizing complete equality. As such, they are meant to address existing democratic deficits and to be transitory towards ensuring women's equal participation in economic decision and policymaking and implementation[40]. In addition to the fact that it is a right for women, women's equal participation in public and political life constitutes a benefit for society as a whole. Studies have shown that women working in politics are no less competent than their male peers (Duflo & Topalova, 2004). Moreover, it has been shown that "not only are women leaders needed to reflect the policy preferences of women voters, but that they may be more effective in doing so"[41]. Women participating on equal terms in public and political life thus ensures that they can pursue policies and decision making which reflects their needs and interests.

Finally, it should be pointed out that a gender-compatible constitution is legally binding on states and is not merely a 'point of view' subject to consensus or disagreement and does not tolerate multiple views. The Iranian woman Fatima Umm Salamah was killed in 1852 and her body dumped in the well after she cried out loud "You can kill me whenever you like, but you cannot stop the

---

40. Euromed Feminist Initiative (EFI-IFE), "Women's Rights and Democracy Building, Promoting a Common Agenda for Equality between Women and Men", Recommendations from Euro-Med conference, Amman, Jordan, 7-8 June 2013, https://goo.gl/vD3b4J.

41. Rohini Pandey and Alexandra Siron will see women in politics: quotas, voter trends, and women's leadership. See the study link on the Internet: http://iknowpolitics.org/sites/default/files/quota.pdf

liberation of women"[42] – it seems that this cry will continue to resonate until women actually succeed in achieving their full equality of rights, which should be at the forefront of entrenching these rights with clear and precise constitutional provisions. This is what should be done. It is our responsibility to all women and men alike as human beings who truly believe in human rights.

References

Beijing Declaration and Platform for Action. (1995). *The fourth world conference on women, annex i Beijing declaration.* http://www.un.org/womenwatch/daw/beijing/pdf/BDPfA%20E.pdf

CEDAW. (1997). Committee general recommendation No. 23, A/52/38.

CEDAW. (2013). General recommendation No. 30 on women in conflict prevention, conflict and post-conflict situations. CEDAW/C/GC/30.

Dahlerup, D. (2005). Increasing women's political representation: new trends in gender quotas. In J. Ballington & A. Karam, (Eds), *Women in parliament: beyond numbers.* International IDEA.

Duflo, E., & Topalova, P. (2004). Unappreciated service: performance, perceptions, and women leaders in India. Poverty Action Lab. http://economics.mit.edu/files/793

European Commission. (2011). *Gender equality in the European Union.* European Union. http://ec.europa.eu/justice/gender-equality/files/brochure_equality_en.pdf

HR/PUB/14/6. (2014). *Reproductive rights are human rights: a handbook for national human rights institutions.* UN Population Fund, Office of the UN High Commissioner for Human Rights, and Danish Institute for Human Rights. http://www.ohchr.org/Documents/Publications/NHRIHandbook.pdf

IACHR. (2015). Legal standards: gender equality and women's rights. *Inter-American Commission on Human Rights.* https://www.oas.org/en/iachr/reports/pdfs/LegalStandards.pdf

Irving, H. (2008). *Gender and the constitution: equity and agency in comparative constitutional design.* Cambridge University Press.

---

42. This was the last phrase uttered by Fatima Umm Salamah who lived in Iran in the 19th century. She was born in 1817 and was known as "Tahra". She defended the issue of equality between men and women and challenged the rules of those days that ruled women in inferiority. She died in 1852 and her body was thrown into a well which was then blocked by stones. See: Training manual on human rights monitoring. Office of the High Commissioner for Human Rights Vocational Training Series No. 7 United Nations New York and Geneva, 2001. p. 84; http://www.ohchr.org/Documents/Publications/training7Introen.pdf

Kedzia, D. (2013). *Guidelines on human rights and the constitution-making*. Publications of the Social Contract Center Cairo.

Palacios Zuolaga, P. (2008). The path to gender justice in the Inter-American court of human rights. *Texas Journal of Women and the Law, 17*(2), 227-295.

Radacic, I. (2008). Gender equality jurisprudence of the European court of human rights. *European Journal of International Law, 19*(4), 841-857. http://www.ejil.org/pdfs/19/4/1663.pdf

Suteu, S., & Draji, I. (2015). *ABC for a Gender Sensitive Constitution*. Euromed Feminist Initiative IFE-EFI. https://www.efi-ife.org/sites/default/files/ABC%20for%20a%20Gender%20Sensitive%20Constitution.pdf

Constitutions

Belgium: http://www.legislationline.org/documents/id/9045

Brazilia: http://english.tse.jus.br/arquivos/federal-constitution

Canadian Charter of Rights and Freedoms: http://laws-lois.justice.gc.ca/eng/Const/page-15.html

Ecuador: http://pdba.georgetown.edu/Constitutions/Ecuador/english08.html

France: http://www.wipo.int/wipolex/en/text.jsp?file_id=179092

Germany (2014): https://www.btg-bestellservice.de/pdf/80201000.pdf

Italy: http://www.jus.unitn.it/dsg/pubblicazioni/costituzione/costituzione%20genn2008eng.pdf

Kenya: http://www.kenyalaw.org/lex/actview.xql?actid=Const2010

Portugal: https://www.constituteproject.org/constitution/Portugal_2005.pdf

Russia: http://www.constitution.ru/en/10003000-01.htm

Spain: https://www.boe.es/legislacion/documentos/ConstitucionINGLES.pdf

South Africa: http://www.justice.gov.za/legislation/constitution/chp02.html

The Islamic Republic of Iran: http://www.iranhrdc.org/english/english/human-rights-documents/iranian-codes/3017-the-constitution-of-the-islamic-republic-of-iran.html?p=7

Tunisia: https://www.constituteproject.org/constitution/Tunisia_2014.pdf

Turkey: https://global.tbmm.gov.tr/docs/constitution_en.pdf

Venezuela: https://venezuelanalysis.com/constitution

Yemen: http://www.refworld.org/pdfid/3fc4c1e94.pdf

10 Women's rights and constitutional implementation in the MENA region: challenges and perspectives

Francesco Biagi[1]

Several constitutional reforms adopted in Middle Eastern and Northern African countries (MENA region) following the Arab uprisings have significantly strengthened the provisions on women's rights and gender equality. The 1996 Moroccan constitution, for example, only granted political rights to women (Article 8), while the new 2011 Moroccan constitution declares that: "The man and the woman enjoy, in equality, the rights and freedoms of civil, political, economic, social, cultural, and environmental character [...]" (Article 19). In Egypt, "equality between women and men in all civil, political, economic, social, and cultural rights" has become an object which the State "commits to achieving" (Article 11(1)). The 2014 Egyptian constitution also declares that "The State commits to taking the necessary measures to ensure appropriate representation of women in the houses of parliament, in the manner specified by the law. It grants women the right to hold public posts and high management posts in the state, and to appointment in judicial bodies and entities without discrimination" (Article 11(2)). In Tunisia, the 2014 constitution states that "All citizens, male and female, have equal rights and duties, and are equal before the law without any discrimination" (Article 21), and that the right to work is "a right for every citizen, male and female" (Article 40). The Tunisian constitution also guarantees "equality of opportunities between women and men to have access to all levels of responsibility and in all fields" (Article 46), and provides that "every male and female voter" has the right to stand for election as President of

1. University of Bologna, Bologna, Italy; francesco.biagi4@unibo.it

How to cite this chapter: Biagi, F. (2018). Women's rights and constitutional implementation in the MENA region: challenges and perspectives. In C. Padovani & F. Helm (Eds), *Rethinking the transition process in Syria: constitution, participation and gender equality* (pp. 143-155). Research-publishing.net. https://doi.org/10.14705/rpnet.2018.21.764

the Republic (Article 74). In Algeria, the February 2016 constitutional reform[2] introduced a provision that stipulates that the State promotes "equality between men and women in the labour market" and "encourages the advancement of women in positions of responsibility in public institutions and administrations, as well as at a company level" (Article 36).

However, in order to assess the sincerity of these innovations, *the process of constitutional implementation* will be decisive. The latter will be undoubtedly extremely complicated, since North Africa and the Middle East is a region in which – more than in other parts of the world – women's rights and the principles of gender equality and non-discrimination have often remained 'on paper'.

In this short paper, I will address some of the most relevant *factors* that may influence the process of constitutional implementation, i.e. (1) the nature of the constitution, (2) the role played by the constitutional courts, (3) the 'limitation clauses', (4) international treaties and conventions on human rights, (5) women's representation in elected institutions, and (6) the social, cultural, and religious context.

1.   The nature of the constitution

The first factor that may deeply influence the process of implementing constitutional provisions concerning women's rights and gender equality relates to the *very nature of the constitution* in question. In particular, it is crucial to verify whether constitutions in the Arab world are considered *legally binding documents*, the *highest laws of the land*, or whether they are merely perceived as *political and/or symbolic texts*, deprived of any legal value. This question is of the utmost importance since only a constitution which is considered the supreme law of the State will be able to effectively protect women's fundamental rights (and more generally human rights).

---

2. Currently, there is not an English version available online of the updated Algerian constitution; quotes are translated from the official French version.

It should be recalled that for a long time, the significance of the constitution in Europe was radically different from the significance that the constitution had in the United States (US). In the US, the constitution has been considered, since the very beginning, the "superior, paramount law" – as it was made clear by the Supreme Court in *Marbury v. Madison* (1803) –, with the consequence that statute laws in contrast with the constitution had to be considered void.

In Europe, on the contrary, the notion of constitution was for a long time deeply affected by the Jacobin ideal of the 'law as the expression of the general will', which denied the normative character of the constitution. The latter was considered a symbolic text, or, in a best case scenario, a political document aimed at regulating the organisation of the branches of government (Blanco Valdés, 1997; García de Enterría, 2006). This idea of the constitution only changed starting from the end of World War II, thanks to the establishment of constitutional courts which regarded constitutions as legally binding texts (Biagi, 2016). In this way, the normativity of the constitution became a "brute fact of the legislator's world" (Stone Sweet, 2000, p. 196).

In the MENA region, the constitutions adopted following the decolonization process were mainly perceived as political and/or symbolic documents. Indeed, once they became independent, many Arab States promulgated constitutions "as an expression of national sovereignty" (Brown, 2002, p. 10), and the role of these texts was "less legal than symbolic or programmatic" (Le Roy, 2012, p. 110).

This notion of the constitution has changed gradually over time. On the one hand, nowadays constitutions are perceived as more legally binding than in the past. An example of this trend towards the normative value of the constitution is given by the fact that the preambles to several constitutions (i.e. Morocco, Syria, Tunisia, Egypt, and Algeria) are classified by the constitutions themselves as constituting an 'integral part' of the constitution in question. This means that these preambles – which proclaim, *inter alia*, the principles of gender equality, non-discrimination, and equal opportunities – constitute a parameter for constitutional review (*bloc de constitutionnalité*).

On the other hand, however, the full recognition of the normative value of the constitution in most of the Arab countries is yet to come. In a similar manner to the role played by European constitutional courts in the last century, Arab constitutional courts, whose powers and competences have been strengthened – as discussed below – may be crucial in clearly recognizing and guaranteeing the normativity and supremacy of the *entire constitution*, with particular attention to the principle of equality and the provisions on fundamental rights and freedoms.

2.   The role played by constitutional courts

Another factor that may influence the process of implementation of the constitutional provisions concerning women's rights and gender equality is given by the role played by constitutional courts. It should be noted that judicial review, generally in the form of constitutional courts and councils, was a common feature in the MENA region even before the Arab uprisings. However, "only a few of the bodies charged with the task [were] viewed as effective defenders of constitutionalism" (Brown, 1998, p. 85). One of the very few exceptions was given by the Egyptian Supreme Constitutional Court, which, during the period from the mid-eighties to the end of the nineties, struck down several laws adopted by the regime, thus seriously challenging Mubarak's government (Moustafa, 2007).

Interestingly enough, the Arab upheavals gave rise to the *emergence and strengthening* of constitutional courts in the MENA region. Jordan and Palestine established a constitutional court for the first time in their history, respectively in 2012 and 2016; Morocco, Syria, Tunisia, and Algeria reinforced the position and the competences of their respective constitutional courts; in Egypt, the Supreme Constitutional Court continues to be an extremely powerful and influential body (Frosini & Biagi, 2015, p. 129).

The most significant novelty is probably given by the *procedural gateways* to the constitutional courts. While in the past the referrals to these bodies mainly came from governmental entities (such as the president of the republic, the speaker of the parliament...), the recent constitutional reforms have widened access by granting to *ordinary courts* the power to challenge the constitutionality of laws before the constitutional courts. This undoubtedly represents a fundamental step, since in this way individuals (including women) can have access – at least indirectly – to constitutional courts. Indeed, thanks to the introduction of concrete constitutional adjudication, when an ordinary judge concludes (either following a request by one of the parties or *ex officio*, depending on the country) that the law that has to be applied to the specific case violates the constitution, he/she must suspend the case and refer a question of constitutionality to the court. This system is therefore likely to increase the likelihood of constitutional courts ruling on the constitutionality of laws that violate the principle of equality (including gender equality) and human rights (including women's rights).

A distinction, however, has to be drawn between the countries that have adopted a 'single filter' system and the countries that have adopted a 'double filter' system. Indeed, some countries (e.g. Egypt and Tunisia) have followed the system that can be found, for example, in Germany, Italy, and Spain, where all courts – including lower courts – can directly refer questions of constitutionality to the constitutional court ('single-filter' system). Other countries (e.g. Jordan and Algeria), on the contrary, have followed the French model, where lower courts have to refer the question of constitutionality to the apex courts (such as the Court of Cassation and the Council of State), which then decide whether to refer the question to the constitutional court ('double-filter' system).

As previously mentioned in Biagi (2017), it should be noted that the French and the Jordanian experiences have shown that the 'double-filter' system can be rather problematic, especially at the outset. In France, during the first year of operation of the *question prioritaire de constitutionnalité*, the Court of Cassation (but not the Council of State) displayed a certain level of "resistance" (Molfessis, 2011, p. 83) when referring questions of constitutionality to the constitutional council. In Jordan, five years after the establishment of the constitutional court, the extremely low number of judgments issued by the constitutional court would appear to be related – amongst other things – to a certain reluctance on the part of the Court of Cassation to refer questions of constitutionality to the constitutional court. The Venice Commission (2011) has underlined that "from the viewpoint of human rights protection, it is more expedient and efficient to give *courts of all levels* access to the Constitutional Court" (p. 18, emphasis added). Therefore, the 'single filter' system seems to be more suitable for guaranteeing protection for women's rights.

3.   The 'limitation clauses'

A factor that might have a positive impact on the process of implementation of the constitutional provisions concerning women's rights and gender equality is given by the 'limitation clauses', i.e. the clauses which are aimed at guaranteeing that the core, the essence of fundamental rights, is not affected by the implementing legislation. These clauses – that can be found, for example, in the Constitutions of Germany (Article 19(2)), South Africa (Article 36) and Kenya (Article 24) – were also included in the Constitutions of Jordan (Article 128(1)), Tunisia (Article 49) and Egypt (Article 92). Their introduction was clearly aimed to overcome the practices of the past, when laws implementing the fundamental rights and freedoms declared by the constitutions often 'hollowed out' those very same rights.

It has been rightly pointed out that the limitation clause contained in the Tunisian constitution is "probably the Arab region's most detailed [one]" (Al-Ali & Ben Romdhane, 2014, n.p.). Article 49 of the Tunisian constitution states that legislation limiting rights can only be adopted if it is "necessary to a civil and democratic society" and "provided there is proportionality between these restrictions and the objective sought". This provision, however, also states that limitations to fundamental rights can be put in place "with the aim of protecting the rights of others, or based on the requirements of *public order, national defence, public health, or public morals,*" (Article 49, emphasis added) which leaves room for potential abuses. The constitutional court will play a key role in assessing whether the core, the essence of fundamental rights (including women's rights), has been violated or not.

4. International treaties and conventions on human rights

Following the Arab uprisings, a number of countries have adopted a noticeably *favourable stance towards international treaties and human rights conventions (including those on women's rights)*. On the other hand however, the *will to preserve national identity (especially in relation to religion)* has thus far prevented their full incorporation into domestic legal systems. These two opposing trends can be easily seen in Tunisia and Morocco.

Tunisia, which has long been at the forefront of the Arab world with respect to women's rights, took another historical step in 2014 when it became the first Arab country to withdraw all its reservations to the Convention on the Elimination of All Forms of Discrimination against Women (CEDAW). At the same time, however, Tunisia decided to maintain a general declaration which states that the country "shall not take any organizational or legislative decision in conformity with the requirements of this Convention where such a decision would conflict with the provisions of Chapter I of the Tunisian Constitution".

Chapter I of the Constitution states – *inter alia* – that the religion of Tunisia is Islam (Article 1). It is to be seen, then, whether the withdrawal of the reservations will be translated into actual laws, or whether the retention of the general declaration will prevent major changes to ordinary legislation from taking place.

In Morocco, Article 19 of the 2011 Constitution stipulates that "the man and the woman enjoy, in equality, the rights and freedoms of civil, political, economic, social, cultural, and environmental character, enounced in this Title and in the other provisions of the Constitution, as well as in the international conventions and pacts duly ratified by Morocco and this, with respect for the provisions of the Constitution, of the immutable values [*constantes*][3] of the Kingdom and of its laws". The 'immutable values' clearly recall Islam, which

---

3. The French 'constantes' is usually translated by the leading literature as 'immutable values'.

is the religion of the State (Article 3 of the 2011 Moroccan constitution). When applying this provision, the judges may base their reasoning on the reference of the constitution to the "international conventions and pacts duly ratified by Morocco", or, alternatively, give greater emphasis to the "immutable values and the laws of the Realm" – which, as noted above, are also expressly enshrined within the constitution. Therefore, it would appear that the constitution permits two diametrically opposed interpretations in relation to the principle of gender equality: one "in favor of universalism", and one "towards conservatism" (Bernoussi, 2012, 2016, p. 225 and p. 705, respectively).

Striking a balance between the respect of international treaties on human rights – and in particular on women's rights – on the one hand, and the preservation of national identity (especially when it comes to religion) on the other, now more than ever represents one of the major challenges for Arab countries.

5.   Women's representation in elected institutions

Securing greater participation by women in political parties and representation in public institutions, and consequently increasing the chances of the effective implementation of the constitutional provisions on gender equality, can contribute enormously to guaranteeing full citizenship for women. This seems to be of the utmost importance in North Africa and the Middle East, where women very often can hardly make their voices heard.

Although they are not immune from criticism, it seems that *electoral gender quotas* can contribute to achieving this aim. Electoral quotas for women are nowadays provided for in a number of Arab countries. In Algeria, for example, thanks to the electoral quota, 26% of the seats of the Lower House are held by women. Electoral quotas for women are provided for also in other countries, such as Egypt, Morocco, and Jordan, but women's representation in Parliament is lower.

In Tunisia, Article 46 of the constitution guarantees "equality of opportunities between women and men to have access to all levels of responsibility and in all domains. The state seeks to achieve equal representation for women and men in elected councils"[4]. This gender sensitive provision is reflected in the electoral legislation. Indeed, the electoral law for parliamentary elections provides for the principle of 'vertical equality' – according to which electoral lists have to be established in such a way to alternate between men and women. Currently, 31% of the seats of Parliament are held by women. Moreover, the electoral law for municipal and regional elections adopted in February 2017 took a further step by providing for the principle of 'horizontal equality' – according to which "political parties will be obliged to respect the equality of sexes, not only in the same list but also between the lists that they present in different constituencies in such a way that if in Constituency A the lead candidate of a list is a man, the lead candidate in Constituency B must be a woman" (Mekki, 2017, n.p.).

It should be noted, however, that an electoral quota *per se* is not enough to guarantee women's representation. This has to be complemented with an electoral system that favors women's representation (it is generally agreed that *proportional systems* are favourable to the election of women and make the quota system work better), and with an *electoral management body* in charge of verifying that the measures aimed at guaranteeing women's participation in elections are respected, i.e. "exemptions from candidacy fees, access to official media, access to public resources, [and] imposing sanctions on the political parties that fail to comply, including elimination of lists that exclude women" (Suteu & Draji, 2015, p. 63).

6.   The social, cultural, and religious context

In spite of the fact that in the past two decades several countries have taken important steps to strengthen women's rights, the path towards creating real

---

4. Translated from the official French text of the 2014 constitution.

equality between men and women in the MENA region is still very long and difficult. The *social, cultural, and religious context* is the factor that – probably more than others – has thus far prevented women from obtaining full citizenship in the Arab world. In particular, for a long time women have been fighting against a patriarchal interpretation of Islamic texts, which have been used to legitimize various legal and social restrictions against them. It has been rightly pointed out that

> "it is necessary to deconstruct this politicized structure and reconstruct it, by relying again on the spirit of the Quranic text, which gives all the possibilities to contextualize the equality between man and women. Therefore, women have to regain what was usurped from them over centuries" (Gaté, 2014, p. 10).

For the moment, resistance to greater gender equality from certain sections of society, political parties, and public institutions is extremely strong, and will not be uprooted easily.

Examples of discrimination against women in Arab societies are boundless. It is emblematic, for example, that at the beginning of October 2016 a member of the Egyptian parliament called for mandatory virginity tests for women seeking university admission. The aim of these tests would be to prevent informal marriages (known as '*gawaz orfy*') between young people who choose to have premarital sex (New York Times, 2016). Another example is given by Morocco, where, on the 23rd of November 2016 (i.e. two days before the International Day for the Elimination of Violence Against Women), a program on state television demonstrated how women could use makeup to cover up evidence of domestic violence, thus helping them to "carry on with [their] daily life", as the host said at the end of the segment (Ait Akdim, 2016, n.p.).

It goes without saying that social and cultural changes cannot be imposed 'from above', although parliaments, governments, courts and all the other public institutions can facilitate these changes. The case of Italy during the sixties is emblematic. In 1961, the Italian constitutional court delivered a judgment (no. 64/1961) in which it declared that Article 559 of the Criminal Code – which only punished women's adultery (and not men's) – did not violate the provisions of the Constitution that guarantee the equality between men and women. Indeed, according to the court, women's adultery – more than men's adultery – could threaten the unity of the family.

Seven years later, in 1968, the Italian constitutional court (judgment no. 126/1968) was asked to re-examine the issue. This time the court decided to strike down the provision of the Criminal Code that punished only women's adultery, stating that the *historical and the social conditions had deeply changed*, and that men and women had to be considered on the same footing within the family and the entire society.

As mentioned at the beginning of this short paper, several constitutional reforms adopted in the MENA region following the Arab uprisings have significantly reinforced the provisions on women's rights and gender equality. Now, it is up to public institutions to respect and implement these provisions, thus spearheading positive changes in Arab societies.

References

Ait Akdim, Y. (2016, December 7). Au Maroc, œil au beurre noir cherche poudre libre pour maquillage de violences. *Le Monde Afrique.* http://www.lemonde.fr/afrique/article/2016/12/07/au-maroc-il-au-beurre-noir-cherche-poudre-libre-pour-maquillage-de-violences_5045016_3212.html

Al-Ali, Z., & Ben Romdhane, D. (2014, February 16). Tunisia's new constitution: progress and challenges to come. *OpenDemocracy.* https://www.opendemocracy.net/north-africa-west-asia/zaid-al-ali-donia-ben-romdhane/tunisia%E2%80%99s-new-constitution-progress-and-challenges-to-

Bernoussi, N. (2012). La Constitution de 2011 et le juge constitutionnel. In *La constitution marocaine de 2011: analyses et commentaires*. Centre d'Études Internationales L.G.D.J.

Bernoussi, N. (2016). Morocco's constitutional court after the 2011 reforms. In R. Grote & T. Röder (Eds), *Constitutionalism, human rights, and Islam after the Arab Spring*. Oxford University Press.

Biagi, F. (2016). *Corti costituzionali e transizioni democratiche*. Tre generazioni a confronto. Il Mulino.

Biagi, F. (2017). The Algerian Constitutional Reform of 2016: a critical analysis. *Global Jurist, 17*(3). https://doi.org/10.1515/gj-2017-0009

Blanco Valdés, R. L. (1997). *Il valore della Costituzione. Separazione dei poteri, supremazia della legge e controllo di costituzionalità alle origini dello Stato liberale*. CEDAM.

Brown, N. (1998). Judicial review and the Arab world. *Journal of Democracy*, 9(4), 85-99. https://doi.org/10.1353/jod.1998.0056

Brown, N. (2002). *Constitutions in a nonconstitutional world. Arab basic laws and the prospects for accountable government*. SUNY Press.

Frosini, J. O., & Biagi, F. (2015). Transitions from authoritarian rule following the Arab uprisings: a matter of variables. In J. O. Frosini & F. Biagi (Eds), *Political and constitutional transitions in North Africa. Actors and factors*. Routledge.

García de Enterría, E. (2006). *La Constitución como norma y el Tribunal constitucional*. Aranzadi.

Gaté, J. (2014). Droits des femmes et révolutions arabes. *La Revue des droits de l'homme*, 6. https://doi.org/10.4000/revdh.929

Le Roy, T. (2012). Constitutionalism in the Maghreb: between French heritage and Islamic concepts. In R. Grote & T. Röder (Eds), *Constitutionalism in Islamic countries. Between upheaval and continuity*. Oxford University Press.

Mekki, N. (2017, March 27). *The law on local and regional elections: a step towards local democracy in Tunisia*. http://www.constitutionnet.org/news/law-local-and-regional-elections-step-towards-local-democracy-tunisia

Molfessis, N. (2011). La résistance immédiate de la Cour de Cassation à la QPC. *Pouvoirs*, 137, 83-99. https://doi.org/10.3917/pouv.137.0083

Moustafa, T. (2007). *The struggle for constitutional power: law, politics and economic development in Egypt*. Cambridge University Press. https://doi.org/10.1017/CBO9780511511202

New York Times. (2016, October 3). *Egyptian politician under fire after recommending mandatory virginity tests*. http://nytlive.nytimes.com/womenintheworld/2016/10/03/egyptian-politician-under-fire-after-recommending-mandatory-virginity-tests/

Stone Sweet, A. (2000). *Governing with judges. Constitutional politics in Europe.* Oxford University Press. https://doi.org/10.1093/0198297718.001.0001

Suteu, S., & Draji, I. (2015). *ABC for a gender sensitive constitution. Handbook for engendering constitution-making.* Euromed Feminist Initiative IFE-EFI.

Venice Commission. (2011). *Study on individual access to constitutional justice.* http://www.venice.coe.int/WebForms/documents/default.aspx?pdffile=CDL-AD(2010)039rev-e

Constitutions

Egypt (2014): https://www.constituteproject.org/constitution/Egypt_2014?lang=en

Germany (1949): https://www.btg-bestellservice.de/pdf/80201000.pdf

Jordan (1952): http://www.refworld.org/pdfid/3ae6b53310.pdf

Kenya (2010): http://www.wipo.int/edocs/lexdocs/laws/en/ke/ke019en.pdf

Morocco (1996): http://unpan1.un.org/intradoc/groups/public/documents/un-dpadm/unpan041912.pdf

Morocco (2011): https://www.constituteproject.org/constitution/Morocco_2011.pdf?lang=en

South Africa (1996): http://www.justice.gov.za/legislation/constitution/chp02.html

Syria (2012): http://www.ilo.org/wcmsp5/groups/public/---ed_protect/---protrav/---ilo_aids/documents/legaldocument/wcms_125885.pdf

Tunisia (2014): https://www.constituteproject.org/constitution/Tunisia_2014.pdf

11 No democracy without gender equality

Maya Alrahabi[1]

The war in Syria has been going on for seven consecutive years. It began with peaceful demonstrations against the tyrant regime for months, then was faced with excessive violence. Many protesters were arrested and tortured brutally, which led to the death of some of them. Many other peaceful protesters were killed by gunshots during demonstrations. It turned into an armed conflict between the regime and the opposition. Several regional powers intervened in the Syrian conflict by supporting parties to the conflict and arming them, even by sending militias. The regime then began the random shelling of cities where those factions were based, which led to a huge number of civilian casualties. The arrests of peaceful civilian activists, especially those who worked in relief of the afflicted areas, continued by the regime. Many were arrested and brutally tortured and killed (there are documented photos for 11,000 detainees who died under torture). Feminist activists were arrested and tortured, some of them were killed and others were tried by anti-terrorism courts and are still in prison. Others escaped outside Syria and are working in the neighbouring countries, or all over the world. Fighters of the Islamic State of Iraq and the Levant (ISIS) began to fly from all over the world to Syria, under the eyes of the whole world, which did not do anything against it until ISIS seized half of Syria, brutally treating Syrian citizens in the areas under its control, especially women who are prohibited from appearing in the public sphere unless they cover their entire bodies, denied education, and work. ISIS applied brutal sanctions on people in their control areas. The international forces (especially USA and Russia) intervened, which has made the conflict more complex and brutal; they bombard cities all over Syria, most victims being civilians. The regime also laid siege on more than

1. Director of "Musawa", Syria; m.rahabi@gmail.com

How to cite this chapter: Alrahabi, M. (2018). No democracy without gender equality. In C. Padovani & F. Helm (Eds), *Rethinking the transition process in Syria: constitution, participation and gender equality* (pp. 157-165). Research-publishing.net. https://doi.org/10.14705/rpnet.2018.21.765

16 cities that were completely cut off from food, medicine, water, electricity, and all the necessities of life. The armed groups lay siege on two cities as well.

As a result, there are 500,000 dead, hundreds of thousands of detainees and disappearances, 4.8 million refugees in neighbouring countries, more than half a million refugees in Europe, and 7.6 million displaced (Syria's population is 23 million) who suffer inhumane and difficult conditions. What can we do, as feminist movements that stand against wars, who believe in peaceful solutions and dialogue as a means to solve any conflict? Certainly the United Nations (UN) Resolution 1325, and related provisions, are guidelines that could be consulted in times of conflicts, along with international humanitarian laws and many others. We should not forget, however, that all the resolutions, conventions, and treaties have been signed under an international patriarchal order that basically legalizes wars by developing controlling regulations in an attempt to designate an ethical system for an intrinsically unethical act. The UN, for its part, does not depart from the authoritarian male standard that still rules the world, as its composition puts the fate of the people in the hands of five member countries in the Security Council. Eventually, any one of them can use the veto right to obstruct justice and the possibility of a people achieving their rights. This applies to all international treaties and conventions issued by the UN, which do not have a binding character on the ground, allowing the religious male political tyrannical systems to manipulate the destinies of their people, especially women, without any oversight or accountability. The UN also allows states to infringe on other states unchecked, perhaps even under cover from the United Nations itself.

So we raised our voice loud against any form of religious male political domination, which is manifested in authoritarian governments and colonial occupation, resulting in devastating violence. We have always stood against war and all forms of violence, calling for pursuing peaceful ways to resolve conflicts and disputes. Our ways of conflict resolution are based on several points:

- The struggle for an active participation of women in all stages of conflict resolution, peace-building, and reconstruction is through adopting the feminist vision of a peaceful world, in which all forms of armed conflicts are abolished.

- The protection of civilians in wars by helping them, especially women, empowering them, and raising their awareness.

- Mobilizing advocates for our just causes by networking with global women's organizations and human rights organizations, and anyone else that could support our just causes.

- Pressure on the influential international powers and organizations to support our just causes and to resolve our conflicts peacefully.

It is worth noting that people's experiences have shown that the involvement of women in peacemaking, at the local and international levels, give peace a greater impact and make it longer lasting. There is a tendency in the international community for the standardization of the role of women as victims of wars seeking peace, any peace, even if the forces of authoritarianism stay in power, which has contributed to further oppression of the people, depriving them of their will. This is not real peace; it is a fragile peace that is based on the balance between internal and external domination forces. The peace that we seek is the lasting and sustainable peace which will only be achieved by changing the structure of the authoritarian state into a democratic modern secular state, based on the principle of equal citizenship, the rule of law, and social justice. A comprehensive, sustainable, just peace will only be achieved by striking a balance between forgiveness and accountability; namely, forgiving others, and holding accountable all of those whose hands are stained with blood, compensating the victims in accordance with the principles of transitional justice. We are seeking to get to that just and comprehensive peace in a transitional phase that is governed by a constitutional declaration, including all the foundations of a modern democratic state, a transitional provision body with an executive and legislative authority that represents all spectrums of the people, an impartial independent judicial authority that is responsible for monitoring and accountability, a transitional justice under which all those who have committed a crime against the people will have a fair trial, and a transitional period which will allow us to work on drafting a permanent constitution for the country that we seek. The Coalition of Syrian Women for Democracy (CSWD) was founded in July 2012, and since then 16 organizations have joined it so far, and from the beginning it has focused on putting forth and promoting engendered constitutional principles to guide the transition towards democracy in Syria. This ongoing work has been supported from the beginning by the Euromed Feminist Initiative in the frame of different programs funded by Sweden and the European Union.

The CSWD has been building on lessons learned from the experiences of other countries. It published a booklet, *Looking Towards a Democratic Constitution* (2012[2]), and recommendations for promoting nonviolent transition towards democracy through engendering constitution building process in Syria[3] from the international conference held on the 10th and 11th of April 2014 in Brussels. It also published the report, *Gendered constitution building process for Syria* (Zakzak, Hjeieh, & Al Rahabi, 2014), and in 2015 some of its members were involved in the reference group for writing the handbook on engendering constitution-making: *ABC for a Gender Sensitive Constitution* (Suteu & Draji, 2015). CSWD has held several conferences about 'Principles of gendered constitution' in partnership with the Euromed Feminist Initiative at local and international levels. The gendered constitutional principles of Syria, and the mechanisms to implement them adopted by the CSWD are:

- Syria is a sovereign, independent, democratic republic based on political pluralism and administrative decentralization, and has the full right to retrieve its occupied territories within the context of the unity of the Syrian land.

- All Syrian citizens, women and men, are united under one national identity encompassing their different ethnic, cultural, and religious belonging. The constitution guarantees respect, equality, gender

2. http://www.efi-ife.org/equality-first-towards-democratic-constitution

3. http://www.efi-ife.org/gendered-constitution-building-process-syria

equality, non-discrimination, as well as the establishment of equal opportunities for all these social components.

- The constitution guarantees the achievement of full equality between women and men in citizenship rights so that both women and men can enjoy their civil, political, social, economic, cultural, and educational rights in all areas of public and family life.

- The constitution prohibits discrimination, whether direct or indirect, against any citizen on the basis of gender, and obliges the State to issue national laws that prevent, prohibit, and criminalize any act of discrimination against women and all forms of violence against them in both private and public life; to annul all discriminatory laws and texts, to lift all the reservations posed on the Convention on the Elimination of All Forms of Discrimination against Women (CEDAW), and to endorse its optional protocol.

- The Syrian constitution is a secular one and explicitly mentions the separation of religion from the State and legislation.

- The people are the source of power. The constitution guarantees representation of Syrian people through free and impartial elections, which are administered by just laws that ensure women's equal participation, achievement of parity between women and men through providing for affirmative actions such as gender quotas and fair representations of all groups.

- The constitution protects the separation of powers and the establishment of regulations that ensure a balanced relationship among them.

- The constitution ensures equal participation of women in public, political, economic, and social life; their equal right to employment and to holding any decision-making position, as well as their equal representation in all designated and elected bodies.

- The sources of legislation are international human rights treaties and agreements, women's rights conventions and resolutions, as well as international human rights laws and principles of social justice and gender equality.

- All international treaties and agreements ratified by the State have supremacy over national legislation. The constitution and national laws comply with international agreements and conventions ratified by the State that protect the political, economic, and social rights of women and men, on top of which is CEDAW.

- The constitution guarantees the right to life and bans the death penalty; it prohibits ill-treatment and abuse of women and men under any circumstances; it explicitly criminalizes all forms of gender-based violence and torture, including rape, and all other forms of abuse and inhumane treatment.

- The constitution protects the independence of the judiciary and the equality of all citizens, women and men alike, before the law and in the law. The constitution also ensures equal access for women and men to legal entities, equality in treatment, and protection against sexual and physical violence, as well as providing compensations for victims of sexual violence within the system of transitional justice.

- The constitution protects the right of women and men to transfer their citizenship to spouses and children.

- The constitution protects freedom of expression, thought, and conscience, as well as participation in decision making through political parties and civil society organizations, including women's rights organizations, and publishing newspapers and other printed materials.

- The constitution guarantees and protects women's and men's equal rights to education, work, property ownership, and inheritance.

- The constitution ensures abolishing or amending all laws conflicting with these principles.

As mentioned in Zakzak et al. (2014), the CSWD has also elaborated mechanisms to implement the above-mentioned gender-sensitive constitutional principles. In this vein:

- The constitution must be written in a gender-sensitive language. The words 'women and men' must be clearly included after phrases like 'all citizens' or 'individuals' to emphasize that women and men are equal in worth, before the law and in the law.

- The constitution must prohibit the legislative authority from revising its articles in a way that negatively affects gender equality or any of the principles of freedom and justice. The constitution also must clearly state that the articles guaranteeing civil rights and freedoms, and equality between women and men, are not subject to change, unless change was intended to emphasize or enrich, in which case the legislative power may amend some articles.

- The constitution must include implementation mechanisms, such as articles and bodies for equality, to ensure it does not remain a declaration of principles. A supreme national body is created to implement and protect women's rights and establish gender equality in all ministries and local institutions and authorities, along with the gender equality committee in the parliament to monitor the implementation of gender equality law and related issues. The principle of gender equality is established clearly and through all governmental plans and programs.

- Current laws must be amended by the legislative authority to agree with all the rights and freedoms protected by the sought constitution. No article or law should stand in opposition to the spirit of the constitution. If any such contradiction is noted, laws must be amended to be compatible with the constitution, and therefore with international agreements on human and women's rights. Feminist organizations and human rights activists must be involved in the process of revising laws and systems and developing civil and criminal laws to ensure justice and eliminate all forms of discrimination and violence against women.

- The national policy focused on education includes all Syrian children in the educational process, especially those who were deprived from it in the past years, as well as focusing on literacy programs and the spread of knowledge and awareness on democracy, human rights, and gender equality in all educational stages and in all media.

- National policies reflect a positive image of women and stand in opposition to social tolerance towards discrimination against women, and mechanisms guarantee the protection of women's rights in reality. The constitution alone cannot protect women from cultural stereotypes and prejudices which continue to marginalize women in obvious or subtle ways.

- Independent civil records are provided for women to further institutionalize the full citizenship of women.

- A clear work table is set for gender equality and all opportunities are sized to emphasize this issue.

- All social components in Syria are involved in establishing gender equality and raising awareness of women's rights on a local level, since even the progressive forces in Syria hesitate on the subject of gender equality and women's rights.

- All feminist and civil society organizations are engaged and actively participate in the preparation for negotiations and the creation of transitional governing bodies. Civil society organizations must have the freedom to work and be properly represented in committees that adopt programs and policies.

- The participation of women in negotiating delegations of Syrian political parties and powers is ensured at all stages.

- The discussions and negotiations pertain during the constitution building period, since it could change the balance of powers through the mobilization of democratic forces.

- Mechanisms must ensure the transparency and fairness of constitutional referendums and all stages of elections, as well the participation of civil society organizations in monitoring the elections.

- The electoral system is a proportional representative one in order to promote gender equality.

- This entire process is connected to democracy, since women's rights are an indivisible part of the international human rights.

References

Suteu, S., & Draji, I. (2015). *ABC for a Gender Sensitive Constitution.* Euromed Feminist Initiative IFE-EFI. https://www.efi-ife.org/sites/default/files/ABC%20for%20a%20 Gender%20Sensitive%20Constitution.pdf

Zakzak, S., Hjeieh, F., & Al Rahabi, M. (2014). *Gendered constitution building process for Syria.* Coalition of Syrian Women for Democracy. http://www.efi-ife.org/sites/default/ files/merged_document_4.pdf?

Section 4.

Testimonies by civil society organizations and Syrian lawyers' internships at the CIRSG and SPGI

Testimonies from civil society organizations that are active between Italy and Syria and that support women and their families facing conflict situations were offered during a 'Civil Society Dialog' held on the occasion of the International Conference. Initiatives promoted by Auxilia, and the representation of Trama di Terre, both long standing IFE-EFI partner organizations, are introduced.

This section also hosts short contributions from two young lawyers who were welcomed by the Center for Gender Studies at the University of Padova during the first six months of 2016 in the context of the Euromed Feminist Initiative IFE-EFI project titled "Supporting the transition towards democracy in Syria through preparing for an engendered constitution building process". Their goal was to widen their knowledge and understanding of international experiences and constitutional processes in relation to fundamental rights of women and men, and of the mechanisms available to enforce such rights enshrined in the law and constitution; all this with a view to contribute to a democratic transition in Syria through supporting a constitution building process inclusive of gender equality and women's rights.

12 How international cooperation and micro-credit allow women to take back their lives: the Auxilia Onlus experience in Syria

Massimiliano Fanni Canelles[1]

The war in Syria is not new. Since March 2011, there have been thousands of victims of a fratricidal conflict that sees the central government of Bashar al Assad opposed by many representatives of various groups, often simply referred to as 'rebels', but within whose ranks deeply different groups clash.

As always when there is a war, it is the civilians who are the first victims. Today in Syria, it is also difficult to get a count on the number of deaths or displaced or missing people. The many eyes of humanitarian organizations focused on the region have denounced over and again the abuses and violations of human rights carried out on all fronts. From rapes of women and girls to the recruitment of children: the situation is a real humanitarian disaster. It is impossible for people whose raison d'être is the respect of human rights, like us at Auxilia Onlus[2], to stand aside. To stay silent. To look the other way.

Our work started from the need to help the victims of the conflict: the first project was the support of children from the Iblib region, the border area between Syria and Turkey, isolated and abandoned by other international organizations. After the first few visits, we found that, as often happens unfortunately, the worst injuries were those suffered by children and women. However, we also noticed that women could be the key to unlocking the situation and could trigger a small positive change.

---

1. Bologna University, Bologna, Italy; presidente.auxilia@gmail.com

2. Onlus stands for 'Organizzazione Non Lucrativa di Utilità Sociale' (not for profit organizations socially oriented); http://www.auxiliaitalia.it/en/foundation.html

How to cite this chapter: Fanni Canelles, M. (2018). How international cooperation and micro-credit allow women to take back their lives: the Auxilia Onlus experience in Syria. In C. Padovani & F. Helm (Eds), *Rethinking the transition process in Syria: constitution, participation and gender equality* (pp. 169-172). Research-publishing.net. https://doi.org/10.14705/rpnet.2018.21.766

We are accustomed to think of women in the Arab world as submissive, hidden, and marginalized. Instead, especially in countries like Syria, there are emancipated women, armed with a strong university education, and who already before the war did not give up their freedom. Furthermore, the conflict may also stimulate those who had not had many opportunities to get out before. It is the women in the Middle East, even in such a fragile situation, who can take action to try to make a terrible situation more *humane.*

The action of Auxilia aims to re-establish a form of stability for the population living in the areas of Iblib and Atma. The cooperation activities encompass different fields, always placing special attention on women's development: a school was created to involve children and reintegrate people who were working in schools before the war, a small health center was opened, becoming a landmark, and women were offered the opportunity to financially care for their families through micro-enterprise projects.

Indeed, these projects deserve further attention. How is it that in the midst of a terrible conflict like the one in Syria, there is room for micro-entrepreneurs? What can you produce with so few resources? How can products be sold and to whom? It is in this context that opportunities arise when international cooperation is structured, designed, and built in an effective way, addressing the needs of the area in which it operates.

In 2013, a project of female micro-entrepreneurship was started. The aim was to provide women from Idlib and Atma sustenance for their families through the production of scarves. Just scarves, an object used by many women around the world. What was special was the point in which they were made: a knot called 'love knot', from which derived the name of the product and the project: *love scarves.* The knot symbolized the precious bond between Italian women and Syrian ones.

At the Women's Center in Atma, we organized a workshop open to all, where we delivered 100 kg of wool, which then increased thanks to some private donations. The production of scarves is particularly suited to the conditions of the area because they can be produced almost anywhere, including in tents or at home. The idea to make women economically independent in Atma was developed together with the Maram Foundation, a British organization that is our partner in Syria. The scarves produced are then imported into Italy and elsewhere where they are sold at charity markets and awareness events. The goal, which has been partially realized, is to transform a refugee camp into an active community where you can work, learn, and grow. In this way, women and Syrian children can begin, slowly, to regain possession of their lives.

It is not the only humanitarian project that we wanted to vigorously carry out in Syria and in the Turkish border. In collaboration with the Department of Human Sciences, University of Trieste, Maram Foundation, and with the support of the Autonomous Region Friuli Venezia Giulia, we have implemented another project, 'Aurora in Syria', which consisted in vocational training, conflict mediation, and reconciliation. Within this frame, we have promoted some courses in various areas: mediation, negotiation, post-traumatic stress disorder, sewing, and knitting. One hundred and fifty refugees of Atma, from 15 to 50 years old and in particular widows, abused women, women with low education, and disabled women, have learned small jobs and strengthened themselves through their participation in the micro-credit activities.

Recently, our activities have increased in order to provide additional support and space for action for Syrian refugees. Al Bayti, which means 'my home', will soon come to life as a female youth center at the orphanage Al Bayti (Reyhanli, Turkey), to provide women of the area a meeting place where they can engage in specific activities and talk. The hope is that it becomes a space where micro-entrepreneurship projects can be carried out thanks to the psychosocial support also offered to participants.

At the same time, we also started the WomenNet project, aimed at creating a local network and support tools for refugee women. In this case, the primary objective is to offer psychological support to cope with the post-traumatic stress disorders that are often, unfortunately, the invisible wounds of war.

Choosing to support women is not a choice like any other, it is not the result of chance but a concrete response to the humanitarian emergency. Women have a fundamental role in every society and even more so in a community plagued by violence that forces them to escape far from home and to face enormous obstacles. Women can turn into an exciting and vital fulcrum. Most women are away from the logic of physical violence, less corruptible, and more sensitive to suffering. This way, even remotely, you can help those who need it most in a concrete way so that the tragedies and bombs of the past will leave room for a safe and bright future.

13 In search of liberty through self-determination: women in need of international protection and violence against women in the contemporary context of globalized migrations

Giulia D'Odorico[1]

Trama di terre (Weave of Lands) is a feminist association[2] set up in 1997 in Imola, in the province of Bologna (Italy), by a group of women from different backgrounds. Most of the founders and the members are of migrant origin. The main purpose of the association is to assert grassroot women's rights while working for concrete political answers to the concerns of women, especially of those who usually remain on the sidelines of the mainstream because of their class, religion, sexual orientation, or ethnicity. The association provides a range of advice and support services to women, such as a cultural center, including a school of Italian language for foreign women, a women's library, an anti-violence center, including two shelters, a housing service for women in need, and a reception project addressed to refugee and asylum seeking women.

The association currently hosts around 30 women, and every year hundreds of women come across Trama in order to find support and help. Furthermore, the association is member of a wide network of institutions, non-governmental organizations, and universities, such as the Euromed Feminist Initiative, aimed at researching women's rights and developing gender-sensitive programs and policies at local, national, and European level. Since 2014, because of the increasing number of women who cross the Mediterranean and then apply for asylum in Italy, the association has been consistently engaged in developing

---

1. Trama di Terre, Imola BO, Italy; giuliadodorico@hotmail.com, info@tramaditerre.org

2. http://www.tramaditerre.org

How to cite this chapter: D'Odorico, G. (2018). In search of liberty through self-determination: women in need of international protection and violence against women in the contemporary context of globalized migrations. In C. Padovani & F. Helm (Eds), *Rethinking the transition process in Syria: constitution, participation and gender equality* (pp. 173-177). Research-publishing.net. https://doi.org/10.14705/rpnet.2018.21.767

---

and implementing gender-sensitive reception measures and tools in order to secure the specific needs of women and girls in refugee contexts. According to the United Nations High Commissioner for Refugees (UNHCR) statistics between January and June 2016, around 115,068 people arrived in Italy (almost the same in 2015: 116,149) (UNHCR, 2016). The number of women increased from 9% in January to 14% in August. The most represented nationalities are Nigeria (around 20%), Eritrea (13%), Sudan (7%), Gambia, Ivory Coast, Guinea (6%), and Somalia (5%). According to the International Organization for Migration (IOM), in 2016 around 3,501 people lost their lives crossing the Mediterranean[3]. This number includes missing people. In particular, Trama di terre is concerned with improving the specific life conditions of women seeking international protection in Italy, taking as a starting point their own words and the life experiences they share with us during the hospitality. Currently, we host 30 women and two children. They come from Cameroun, Eritrea, Mali, Nigeria, and Somalia. The association financially sustains two of them, since they have been excluded from the official aid system: it provides them with immediate relief through housing, health and economic support, legal aid, and psychosocial care along with the asylum procedure.

In addition, the association advocates with politicians, health services, training centers, universities, etc., to improve aid efficiency at local, regional and national level, and to take their specific needs into account. All the activities are developed with the aim of designing and implementing long-term solutions for an adequate refugee protection system within a specific gender-sensitive and cross-cultural perspective. However, we recognize that in Italy the refugee system is still managed according to an emergency logic, as if the refugee fluxes were temporary – this is not the case as the data related to migration flows shows very clearly. Moreover, adequate and forward-looking international migration policies to face the refugee crisis are completely missing, as the recent UN summit showed, as well as the raising of walls across Europe. As of today, six walls have been built across European borders; and Europe has spent 1.7 billion on them.

---

3. http://migration.iom.int/europe/

In 2016, some international reports, such as those of Amnesty International (2016), the Women's Refugee Commission (Cosgrave et al., 2016), and Save the Children (Coppola & Lo Iacono, 2016), described how the majority of women and girls seeking asylum in Europe experienced multiple forms of violence against women throughout their life-course, in their countries of origin, transit, and arrival. In Trama, we try to create a space where women may share their experiences of violence and find support. Most women tell us about the extremely gender discriminating context they were born and grew up in. Most of them did not have any access to formal education or sexual and reproductive services. Some were forced into early marriage – even several times – with older men, and this practice always includes marital rape and unwanted pregnancies. Some others were forced into military service, including different forms of exploitation, torture, and sexual harassment, such as in the case of Eritreans. Other women, like the Somali we meet, fled war contexts dominated by religious fundamentalist groups, where women suffered rape or extreme violence by official/unofficial armed groups. Many women are at risk while they are traveling to Europe, in particular in Libya, where they are at the mercy of traffickers, camp guardians, and official as well as unofficial armed groups. Most women reported being held in private houses and jails against their will, while others have been forced to work without remuneration or to prostitute themselves in the so-called 'connection houses'. Some women have been allowed on board to cross the Mediterranean only by 'accepting' to be raped by the traffickers. Even in the transit and reception centers, they can face violence. They often do not have the opportunity to meet experienced and gender-trained personnel in reception centers. In addition, there are no sex-segregated facilities and female specific-shelters. Most of them declare that they feel at high risk of – or in some cases that they have experienced – sexual molestation or sexual coercion. Moreover, sexual and reproductive health care services are not always immediately accessible. This could prevent the transmission of Human Immunodeficiency Virus (HIV) and sexually transmitted infections or offer access to safe and legal abortion, especially if they suffered rape during the journey.

One of the main issues that is questioning our daily work with women is the trafficking and sexual exploitation of many women asylum seekers. Most of them are of Nigerian origin. Between January and June 2016, around 3,529 women of Nigerian origin arrived in Sicily crossing the Mediterranean from North Africa. We can presume that most of them experienced trafficking or various forms of exploitation[4]. Later, in case sexual exploitation happens in Italy, women risk facing serious repercussions if they denounce their traffickers, who may have access to the existing special program for victims of trafficking (ex Art.18 Dlgs 286/98 ed ex Art.13 L. 228/2003). According to Save the Children (Coppola & Lo Iacono, 2016), in Italy, around 1,225 women and girls entered this program. Note that 80% of victims are of Nigerian origin.

Many others have access to reception measures within the asylum system. Trama is hosting six Nigerian women aged between 19 and 27. All of them have been trafficked and many have been forced into prostitution in Libya. They are still at risk of sexual exploitation in Italy and across Europe. This situation challenges our practices of reception, especially in terms of women's safety and legal support. To conclude, contemporary migration flows challenge our daily work as well as the Italian refugee protection system, while encouraging us to develop adequate measures, tools, and long-term aid policies, with a specific focus on the situation of women and young girls and the different forms of violence they may suffer. We urge the asylum system to recognize women the right to claim asylum based on Violence-Against-Women (VAW), as well as to develop more policies to effectively protect the rights of women seeking asylum.

References

Amnesty International. (2016, January 18). *Female refugees face physical assault, exploitation and sexual harassment on their journey through Europe*. https://www.amnesty.org/en/latest/news/2016/01/female-refugees-face-physical-assault-exploitation-and-sexual-harassment-on-their-journey-through-europe/

---

4. http://www.cittalia.it/images/Position_Paper_NoTratta_DEF.pdf

Coppola, V., & Lo Iacono, E. (2016). *Piccoli schiavi invisibili. I minori vittime di tratta e sfruttamento: chi sono, da dove vengono e chi lucra su di loro.* Save The Children Italia. https://www.savethechildren.it/cosa-facciamo/pubblicazioni/piccoli-schiavi-invisibili

Cosgrave, J., Hargrave, K., Foresti, M., Massa, I. et al. (2016). *Europe's refugees and migrants. Hidden flows, tightened borders and spiralling costs.* ODI. https://www.odi.org/sites/odi.org.uk/files/resource-documents/10887.pdf

UNHCR. (2016). *September, country update Italy.* http://data.unhcr.org/mediterranean/country.php?id=105

14 Learning about gender policies: my experience at the University of Padova

Roula Baghdadi[1]

The course *Gender Politics and the Welfare State in the European Union*, offered by Prof. Lorenza Perini at the Department of Law, Politics, and International Studies, was valuable for me in many aspects. Since the beginning of the course, I started to reconsider my knowledge and information about women's rights and gender equality. I learned how important it is for defenders of women's rights to be fully informed and knowledgeable about the equality that needs to be applied, and how gender equality relates to the constitution, laws, social systems, economics, and security. All too often, this formally recognized equality in many European constitutions and laws does not actually influence women's lives in these communities. Sometimes the society finds ways to violate this equality, and the law allows that to happen. Perhaps we are still living in a patriarchal society, and achieving real equality needs certain conditions beforehand.

After this course, I started to analyze and consider facts and information from a better informed and more comprehensive gender perspective. As for the research work we were invited to carry out as part of our commitment, it was one of the most important components of this course. I developed my own research around the theme *Women's Human Rights*, and this took about three months. In that context, I tried to explain how important it is to focus on the fact that women's rights are an indispensable part of human rights, and an international issue that is beyond the cultural and religious practices and beliefs of any particular community. I would like to mention something related to my Syrian community in this regard: that all Syrian political parties view women rights as a secondary issue. At the same time, unfortunately, even some human rights defenders in Syria hold a relatively similar attitude. I am currently preparing research about

1. Equal Citizenship Center, Damascus, Syria; rolla.bg1981@gmail.com

How to cite this chapter: Baghdadi, R. (2018). Learning about gender policies: my experience at the University of Padova. In C. Padovani & F. Helm (Eds), *Rethinking the transition process in Syria: constitution, participation and gender equality* (pp. 179-180). Research-publishing.net. https://doi.org/10.14705/rpnet.2018.21.768

women's rights under authoritarian regimes, taking the Syrian regime as an example to further explore the challenges related to fostering gender equality in conflict and non-democratic situations.

The Interdepartmental Center for Gender Studies at the University of Padova offered me the opportunity to attend several conferences, where I shared my knowledge and experiences with other activists and feminists from Brazil, Turkey, Argentina, Ecuador, Bangladesh, and Italy.

Furthermore, during my stay in Italy, for five months, I traveled around the country and met many generous and open-minded activists and members of political parties. I learned a lot about Italian culture, history, politics, and economy; about the challenges the Italian women face, and how they fight injustice in their own communities. As a Syrian, in the past I did not have many opportunities to attend such workshops and conferences because of visa issues. Fortunately, after getting an Italian visa, I was allowed to travel to Berlin, Brussels, Moscow, and Paris, where I met unique people and had great experiences.

Finally, I would like to thank Initiative Féministe Euromed - Euromed Feminist Initiative (IFE-EFI) and Equal citizenship center for offering this scholarship and opportunity to me; and to thank the Center for Gender Studies in Padova which gave me the opportunity of attending this course. Now, I have rejoined my advocacy group in Syria – Equal Citizenship Center (ECC) – and I am enrolled in a Master degree in International Law at Beirut Arab University (BAU). I am currently preparing my thesis on "The Legal Framework of Sexual Violence Against Woman in Syria" and I am planning on graduating in summer 2018.

15 Women's role in peace processes: reflections from my internship experience

Yousef Razouk[1]

During our internship to Padova we attended several courses, offered in English, about women's human rights and gender politics, the European Union (EU), and human rights and international justice.

With regard to women's human rights, such courses provided "theoretical, conceptual and methodological analysis of the issues that the UN has increasingly considered as part of the political agenda of human rights in relation to the status of women and decision making; [a conceptualization] that led to the consolidation of certain guidelines [and] policies"[2], and informed our analysis of the Convention of the Elimination of all kinds of Discrimination Against Women (CEDAW).

For what concerns European law and human rights, the courses we attended provided important knowledge of the fundamental texts of EU Laws (particularly the EU Charter of fundamental rights).

While in relation to gender politics and the welfare state in the EU, we studied the historical development of the concept of gender, and the subsequent processes and experiences that had been feeding the knowledge of gender equality; also, we have come to appreciate the mechanisms about how to get access to a gendered mentality and perspective.

We studied the case of reproductive rights: from acknowledging international mobilizations raising their voices to get access to the right to abortion, to

1. Equal Citizenship Center, Damascus, Syria; you.razouk@gmail.com

2. http://en.didattica.unipd.it/off/2017/LM/EP/EP1980/000ZZ/EPP3050113/N0

How to cite this chapter: Razouk, Y. (2018). Women's role in peace processes: reflections from my internship experience. In C. Padovani & F. Helm (Eds), *Rethinking the transition process in Syria: constitution, participation and gender equality* (pp. 181-184). Research-publishing.net. https://doi.org/10.14705/rpnet.2018.21.769

abortion being considered a controversial issue to the degree that we have not heard of any electoral candidate discuss the right to abortion during his/her electoral campaign. Also, analyzing international statistics related to the abortion, I have noticed that the countries which are intensively mixed with the religious socio-cultural background are extremely influenced by these religious beliefs to the degree of considering the very discussion of the topic a taboo.

Finally, for what concerns international justice and human rights, we critically investigated the trajectory of the evolution of the recognition and promotion of social rights in Europe, considering in particular the interactions and intersections between the EU and the Council of Europe.

I also took a two module course that lasted six days (18-23 April 2016) and focused on training for international electoral observers. The aim of the training was to deepen and enhance our theoretical and practical knowledge about the process of observing elections and to provide relevant tools and skills to perform the role in diverse situations.

While in Padova, I also attended several conferences and events, which were extremely useful to share my own experience and getting more details about other countries' realities and situations.

In the context of the course *Gender Politics and the Welfare State in the European Union,* offered by Prof. Lorenza Perini at the Department of Law, Politics and International Studies, I made a presentation about 'Gender and Elections' as an introduction to the importance of gender parity and women's participation in public life. There I discussed two quota types, compulsory and voluntary, and linked them to the electoral systems. Finally, I presented non-quota measures to support women's contributions in political life. All this stressing the crucial role of political parties as gatekeepers in the sharing of relevant and decision-making positions. In that presentation, I reported, as an example, the fact that in Syria the percentage of female parliaments in the legislature is 13% and it is a low percentage if related to the fact that the women comprise approximately half the population in Syria[3]. So, it would be important to allocate a compulsory quota for women as 'reserved seats', no less than 40%, and it is better to give constitutional protection to this measure.

Besides acknowledging the importance of this internship for my personal and professional carrier, in this context I would also like to make some remarks on women's roles in peace processes. We should always keep in mind that women are actually crucial stakeholders in peace building and democratic reform, and yet they are too sidelined because of the entrenched gender based discrimination (DPI, 2012, p. 6); that they protect the coherence of their families despite the tragic impact of conflicts on their domestic and social lives, and that they struggle to maintain a measure of stability during the displacement. Therefore, we should never deny women's immense capacities to exceed the sadness, and to build new hopes in the aim of securing safe futures for their families and communities (DPI, 2012, pp. 11-12).

In the end, I believe that, when it happens, engaging women in the resolutions of conflict has led to more positive and lasting outcomes, which are increasing the inclusivity, increasing the legitimacy of the process by making it more representative and reflective of the wider affected population and future society, and strengthening the ability to prioritize sustainable stability, democratic process, and peacemaking over the sharing of power and distributing political positions (DPI, 2012, pp. 30-31).

We all know that talking about involving women and gender considerations in peace processes is much easier than implementing it in reality: despite international standards that have led to radical changes in language and in the approach of the international community, little results have yet been seen in practice (DPI, 2012, p. 33).

---

3. World bank data https://data.worldbank.org/indicator/SG.GEN.PARL.ZS?locations=SY&view=chart. However, it is worth noting that according to the official website of the Syrian parliament, the percentage is approximately (11.6%) http://www.parliament.gov.sy/arabic/index.php?node=212#

All I have said also relates to women's roles in peace processes in the Syrian situation: Syrian women – both those who have stayed inside the country and those who were forced to flee because of the war – are struggling for the survival of their families and to protect their children. Yet, even now, they are still under-represented at all levels and at all stages of the peace process. It would be time, for all parties in the Syrian conflict, external and internal, to stop marginalizing the role of Syrian women, because without them sustainable stability and democratic life would be extremely difficult to achieve.

Finally, I want to conclude this short note by mentioning that studying comparative politics and policies, and adopting a comparative approach, has been so important in providing me with new ideas about possible methods and solutions to be applied in Syria; at the same time, it is really important to mention that there is no 'one size fits all' solution, as each society and conflict has its own unique features (DPI, 2012, p. 10).

Reference

DPI. (2012). *The role of women in conflict resolution: DPI roundtable meeting Çirag̃an Palace, Istanbul.* Democratic Progress Institute. http://www.democraticprogress.org/wp-content/uploads/2012/11/DPI-Roundtable-The-Role-of-Women-in-Conflict-Resolution1.pdf

World bank data. https://data.worldbank.org/indicator/SG.GEN.PARL.ZS?locations=SY&view=chart

Author index

www.ingramcontent.com/pod-product-compliance
Lightning Source LLC
Chambersburg PA
CBHW031810190326
41518CB00006B/268